Praise for *The Dynamic Great Lakes*

In her cautionary book, environmental activist and professor Spring enthusiastically explores the Great Lakes, and clearly explains why they should be protected.

—**Book Sense** Nov 22 2003

This is intriguing stuff for adults, but the straightforward presentation also lends itself to use in schools.

—Peter Wild **U.S. Water News**

Every library should have this book.

—Stan Lievense, retired fish biologist MDNR

The Dynamic Great Lakes by Barbara Spring is an excellently written, insightfully presented and engaging guide. Chapters cover how the Great Lakes were formed, their physical characteristics and the history of their changes, problems that affect them today and offered solutions and more.

—**The Midwest Book Review**

Worth reading if for no other reason than that the writing is masterfully done…reminded me a little of Rachel Carson's *Silent Spring*.

—Jonathon David Masters, **www.booktrees.com**

This is an impressive little book. Not quite 110 pages long, it's a read of about an hour or so. The author has, however, managed to jam it full of facts and information about the Great Lakes. The author also sprinkles a strong environmental ethic throughout the book coupled with the belief that the democratic process can make a difference.

—Bob Gross, **The Oakland Press**

Spring's handy 108-page primer about the Great Lakes provides the curious with a solid overview of the lakes including their history, physical characteristics, denizens and the threats facing them, particularly from invasive species and pollution.

—Dave LeMieux, **The Muskegon Chronicle**

Spring consulted a number of biologists, geologists and other environmental experts, and translated their jargon into easy-to-understand language.

—*Kentwood News, Tuesday, November 19, 2002*
by TONYA SCHAFER

This is a fascinating and informative read about the ever-changing Great Lakes. It's packed with in-depth history and ecology. Do you know about the disastrous zebra mussel invasion? The whiting effect? Read it to find out and to find out what you can do to help the Great Lakes.

—Libbey, **Gumball Bookstore**

Incredibly informative. Very well done.

—Maria Goddard, Whitefish Point Shipwreck Museum Store

The book is a convenient reference to keep on board or to read up on during the winter to increase your ability to take out-of-town clients on lakeshore tours.

—**Great Lakes Boating**, December 2002

Although my background in limnology is fairly broad, I found that the amount of knowledge that I have gained after reading this book was plentiful. If you are looking for a book that can help you grow as an angler, a scientist or an environmentalist, pick up *The Dynamic Great Lakes* now.

—Rodney Hsu, *Fishing With Rod* (7/9/2002)

Spring's book has resonated with readers, who appreciate its user-friendly descriptions of Great Lakes phenomena.

—Charlie Misner, events coordinator
at The Bookman in Grand Haven.

One of the unique characteristics of the compact book is that it is written in a language devoid of esoteric explanations. The eight chapters of the book reflect the author's teaching and journalistic aptitudes in knowing how to unravel the mystery of the Great Lakes and the many painful dangers they have faced and continue to face.
—N. Goldman, **Bookideas**

The Dynamic Great Lakes

By
Barbara Spring

Independence Books
Baltimore

Third printing

ISBN: 1-58851-731-4
PUBLISHED BY INDEPENDENCE BOOKS
www.independencebooks.com
Baltimore

Printed in the United States of America

Acknowledgments

I wish to acknowledge Chuck Pistis of Sea Grant who supplied timely information on zebra mussels, freshwater sponges and other phenomena. For the chapter on geology, Chilton Prouty, M.S.U. geologist provided information on the work of glaciers in our area. Donald Hall and Mark Luttenton, both educators and researchers on Grand Valley State University's research vessel Angus, welcomed me aboard to observe their laboratory work on Lake Michigan and environs. For information about the Isle Royale redfin lake trout I am thankful and for Bill Deephouse an enthusiastic fish biologist from the Michigan Department of Natural Resources and also Stan Lievense, now retired from the DNR, who located new information on Lake Ontario for me. For the sections on shore ice and dune succession Earl Wolf and the late Sandy McBeath, educators at Hoffmaster State Park Visitor's Center helped by providing hard to get information and answering many questions. Edward L. Mills, Director of the Cornell Biological Field Station answered many questions via e-mail. For N. Scott Momaday, Pulitzer Prize winning author, who taught me the importance of landscape, I am grateful for inspiration.

I am also grateful to my husband Norm Spring who has carried home many of the Great Lakes' finny denizens for my perusal. He showed me that the democratic process really works in the campaign to ban DDT. I am also grateful my father, E. Paul Reineke, a research scientist at M.S.U., left me with a deep respect for nature and its processes.

Table of Contents

Introduction

The story of the Great Lakes is the story of great changes as well as great mistakes.

Formed by Ice Age glaciers that covered much of the Earth then melted back north four times, the Great Lakes in their present form are rather young: 3,000 years, if measured against the age of planet earth. And the Great Lakes continue to change year by year, month by month, week by week, day by day and hour by hour.

The Great Lakes are dynamic bodies of water; we know that lake levels rise and fall as they always have done. Building too close to the water is not wise. This is a natural change, but other changes have been caused by the people inhabiting its watersheds and even beyond the Great Lakes watersheds.

Over the last 200 years, the most rapid changes in the Great Lakes have occurred due to human activities. Some species became extinct while others nearly so. We have learned that with knowledge of how ecology works we have the ability to correct mistakes made in the past.

Some creatures sensitive to pollution are indicators of a healthy environment: mayflies, lake trout, and the American bald eagle for example. With the ban on DDT, eagles are no longer endangered in the lower United States. There are still problems to be solved: exotic species such as the zebra mussel; the loss of wetlands and dunes; and pollutants that reach the lakes through air, earth and water. Tumors in zooplankton have shown up in Lake Michigan.

The Dynamic Great Lakes will show how these freshwater seas have changed and continue to change through natural and man made causes.

1

The Dynamic Great Lakes

"Everything is connected to everything else."
–Barry Commoner

The Great Lakes are a flowing river of seas left behind by Ice Age glaciers and are nearly twenty percent of the world's supply of fresh surface water; the world's greatest freshwater system. The Great Lakes look and behave like oceans because of their great size. Together, the Great Lakes cover an area equal to Scandinavia and have a coastline of 11,232 miles including connecting channels, mainland, and islands. Their shoreline is equal to almost 45 percent of the circumference of the earth.

Their waters descend from highest, coldest, and northernmost Lake Superior through the St. Mary's River and the Soo Locks to fill Lakes Michigan and Huron, then flow through the St. Clair River and Lake St. Clair and the Detroit River into Lake Erie, then down the Niagara River and Niagara Falls into Lake Ontario. Like water spilling from a series of basins, from higher to lower, the water follows gravity running a thousand more miles from the outlet of Lake Ontario through Canada's St. Lawrence River dotted with more than 1,800 islands until their freshwater reaches and mingles with the Atlantic Ocean's saltwater.

Their waters support an array of life that has evolved over thousands of years. These freshwater seas, the Great Lakes, have been exploited and have received the fallout of modern industry and agriculture. They have been invaded by exotic species. As a result, extinctions of freshwater life are taking place rapidly.

According to Anthony Ricciardi, a biologist at Dalhousie University in Nova Scotia, "A silent mass extinction is occurring in our lakes and rivers. North American temperate freshwater ecosystems are being depleted of species as rapidly as rain forests."

As startling as this statement is, it is no surprise to scientists who have been studying the Great Lakes. But with knowledge and the will to correct problems through the democratic process, it is possible to reverse this trend. The story of bald eagles around the Great Lakes is an example.

Return of the Eagles

High above the sand dunes in West Michigan, a pair of American bald eagles cavort; they dart, dive and swirl through the air at dizzying heights. Suddenly one of them turns on its back and they grasp talons spinning into a daring, cart wheeling free fall toward earth. They unlock talons and flap their powerful wings, flying upward at the last instant before hitting the ground. This, their courtship ritual, will bond the two eagles together for life.

Today, bald eagles are seen around the Great Lakes more and more often, but in 1978, these magnificent birds were threatened. Threatened with extinction. Their eggs never hatched since pesticides that lingered in the environment long after they were sprayed to kill insects magnified in Great Lakes food pyramids. The eagle is at the peak of the food pyramid and its favorite food is fish. This makes the eagle an environmental indicator; a measuring stick of how well the whole ecosystem is faring. Where the ecosystem is healthy, eagles can live and raise their young

Since DDT was banned in 1972, the nesting eagle population has tripled. Eagles were a common sight around the Great Lakes in the days when our founding fathers chose it for our national emblem. In those days, eagle nests could be found about fifteen miles apart all around the Great Lakes. The eagles scavenged fish they found washed up on the beach, or snatched them out of the water in their hook like talons. They built their large untidy nests in tall white pines and returned to them year after year. Gradually the eagles retreated to wilderness areas as cities and factories encroached upon the eagle's habitat in the last two centuries. Today the eagle is protected, but some still are shot illegally.

Eagles are Indicators of a Healthy Ecosystem.

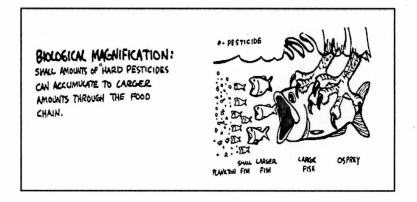

The credit for this cartoon goes to Ozz Warbach

With the widespread use of DDT after Word War II, eagles became an endangered species in the United States with the exception of Alaska, where they are abundant, and Hawaii where they do not live. The bald eagle population around the Great Lakes was especially hard hit. We received an early warning that all was not well in the Great Lakes from the eagle. After eagles fed upon Great Lakes fish day after day, long lasting poisons such as DDT built up in their bodies causing the female to lay eggs without enough calcium. As a result, the eggshells were too thin and broke open before the embryos could hatch. When people became aware of the damage long lasting pesticides such as DDT were causing, legislation was passed to ban these chemicals. DDT was banned in Michigan in 1969 and banned nationally in 1972. In 1975, only six pairs of eagles were nesting in Michigan. In the 1980s, bald eagles nesting near the Great Lakes reproduced at about half the rate of bald eagles inland indicating the presence of toxic chemicals. Today, the eagles' populations have become healthier. By 1994, 260 pairs of eagles nested in Michigan and 255 young were fledged. There were no deformed young as compared to four deformities (crossed bills and club feet) in 1993.

The growing eagle population and lack of deformities in its young shows that the ecosystem is purging itself of DDT and like chemicals. According to wildlife ecologist Stanley Temple of the University of Wisconsin, the return of the eagles and other raptors, including peregrine falcons and ospreys "is due almost wholly to the ban on chlorinated hydrocarbon pesticides." These include: DDT (the number one offender), DDE, deildrin and its derivatives, and polychlorinated bipheynl (PCB). In 1994, the U. S. Fish and Wildlife Service changed the eagle's status from endangered to threatened. The eagle's return is heartening. Their return shows that where people use the democratic process to pass good legislation such as the banning of DDT, some mistakes made in the past can be corrected.

In 2003 there were 3461 bald eagles reported in Michigan, compared with 990 in 2002 and 1510 in 2001, according to Ray Adams, Research Director of the Kalamazoo Nature Center.

Basic to any understanding of life on Earth is the food pyramid. A simplified model of the food pyramid, an approximation of the way living things behave in nature, shows 1,000 pounds of phytoplankton which produces 100 pounds of zooplankton which yields ten pounds of fish which could add one pound to a human.

Trophic Levels

Trophic levels are any of the feeding levels that energy passes through as it continues through the ecosystem. All energy in a living system originates with the sun.

From sunlight and nutrients dissolved in water, phytoplankton or algae, produce food. They are called a fountain of energy, for they multiply rapidly on sunny days producing food to fuel other living things and release oxygen in a process called photosynthesis. They form the broad base of the food pyramid in water. In the Great Lakes the trophic levels are as follows: the first trophic level are the phytoplankton at the base of the pyramid, the most numerous form of life and without them, no other life could exist in water. For example, thousands of types of diatoms, single-celled producers with hard shells of silica, green algae, blue-green algae, and dinoflagellates, with hair like structures that allow them to move, among many other species of phytoplankton, are the most numerous forms of life as they are in any body of water.

On the next trophic level some common zooplankton in the Great Lakes are: copepods such as Cyclops, microscopic protozoans such as amoebas and paramecium, cladocerans such as daphnia, commonly called water fleas, amphipods and rotifers. Some species of zooplankton migrate up and down the water column daily influenced by light, season, and temperature.

On the next level some common larger plankton lacking backbones are called macro invertebrates: in deep water diporeia sometimes called freshwater shrimp and mysis oculata relicta (opossum shrimp) are numerous along with oligochaetes (freshwater worms) and larvae of midges (chironomids). In shallow protected water one might find leeches, fingernail clams, snails, and larvae of mayflies and caddis flies.

On the next level forage fishes such as bloaters, sculpins, emerald shiners, lake herring, sticklebacks and juvenile stages of other fish serve as food for larger fish.

Energy moves through the next trophic level: predator fishes such as yellow perch, lake whitefish, walleye, and various types of trout and salmon.

At the peak of the pyramid are fish eating mammals, man, bears, otters and mink and fish eating birds: American bald eagles, herring gulls, ospreys and cormorants.

Within every body of water, chemicals such as nitrogen and phosphorous travel from the environment to phytoplankton and zooplankton and then back to the environment again. Water dissolved chemicals become part of living tissue. If a chemical such as DDT is in water, it becomes part of living tissue and increases with each step up the food pyramid. When plants and animals die, bacteria and molds recycle their nutrients back into the water in a process called decay.

Bacteria and molds transform dead plants and animals into compounds such as nitrates and phosphates that plants then use to produce food. Without water and oxygen producing phytoplankton and green plants on land, life on Earth as we know it would not be possible.

Food Chains in Water Are Long

Food chains in water are long, much longer than food chains on land; therefore chemicals become more concentrated as energy (and pollutants) move through it. Fish eating birds such as bald eagles, ospreys, cormorants and herring gulls suffered the consequences.

The near demise and then the recovery of the bald eagle and other fish eating birds is an example of change caused by humans. Humans caused the problem and then reversed it before it was too late by banning DDT and like pesticides in the U.S. and Canada.

Extinctions destroy the integrity of ecosystems.

An example of natural change is illustrated by how the lakes were formed over millennia by tremendous forces of nature.

18

2

How the Great Lakes Were Formed

"In wildness is the preservation of the world."
–Henry David Thoreau

In comparison with the age of the Earth, the Great Lakes are quite young. While planet Earth is about 4.5 billion to 5 billion years old, the five Great Lakes were beginning to emerge 10,000 years ago and have only existed as we know them today for the past 3,000 years or so. The five Great Lakes were formed in the last part of the Great Ice Age or the Pleistocene Era as great moving mountains of ice called glaciers melted.

Imagine that one year equals one minute on Planet Earth's Calendar:

January: Earth is formed
February: Earth's crust is formed; Precambrian era
March-June: Saltwater seas formed; Paleozoic era
August: First life formed in the seas
November: the earliest fossils formed
Mid December: dinosaurs roamed the land
After mid December: eagles fly through the air
Late December: mammals roam the planet
End of December: the last day of the last week of the year during the Pleistocene era, 2,500,000 years ago, human beings began to inhabit planet Earth. In the last few minutes, the last of the glaciers melt and the Great Lakes emerge.

What the Precambrian Era Gave Us

Five sixths of all time was during the Precambrian Era: the time when Earth's Crust was formed. The Earth shook and rumbled, volcanoes erupted molten rock, hot lava flew high into the air and flowed, creating land masses as the molten rock cooled and hardened.

The volcanoes formed the hard bedrock that can still be seen today in parts of the Great Lakes basin, especially on the northern shore of Lake Superior where it forms the backbone of the continent. This ancient rock backbone is the Canadian Shield, or the Laurentian Shield. The Laurentian Mountains were once active volcanoes that eroded over the ages by ice, running water, and wind to their present shapes: hills and small mountains. These rocks formed more than 500 million years ago by the volcanic heat and pressure during the Precambrian era are among the most ancient rocks found on Earth and are also found on Minnesota's Lake Superior shoreline and also underlie the northern edge of Lake Huron as well as the Keweenaw Peninsula in Michigan.

The Precambrian era laid the bedrock, a strong foundation for other events to build upon.

What the Paleozoic Era Left Behind

During the Paleozoic era, saltwater seas covered much of the middle part of North America, including the part we call the Great Lakes region, as the land flooded again and again for 230 million years. During this time, ancient forms of life such as algae, zooplankton, fishes, shellfish and corals, lived and died in these warm, shallow salt water seas leaving their fossil remains behind. In some places there are still fossil reefs formed by ancient corals that died leaving their durable limestone formations in the Great Lakes.

Since corals do not grow in freshwater we know these reefs are ancient remnants of the Paleozoic epoch. The Petoskey stone is the fossil of a coral. When polished, the Petoskey stone shows a honeycomb pattern that was once a living colony of sea animals. The fossil corals belong to types of coral that are extinct. Another type of common fossils found on Great Lakes beaches are the crinoids.

Today people find fragments of their round or tube-shaped stems. Crinoids resembled sea lilies, but like corals were really marine animals. Attached to the sea floor by a stem sometimes 70 feet long with food gathering fronds at the top, crinoids swayed to and fro with the currents.

Sometimes people find the imprint of a fish or the imprint of trees and ferns that are now extinct. Great deposits of the shells of microscopic algae called diatoms are widespread around the Great Lakes as well as coccoliths.

Coccoliths, another microscopic form of phytoplankton, have shells of calcium carbonate that often contain a drop of oil; the fossils of coccoliths build up beds of chalk and limestone. Limestone underlies much of the Great Lakes basin. Fossils of plant and animal life, brachiopods, and mollusks that once lived in a salt-water sea lie on the bottom of the Great Lakes basin and are sometimes washed up on the beaches of the freshwater Great Lakes.

In addition to fossils, we also find great deposits of limestone, dolomite, gypsum and salt beds underground. Coal, oil and gases in the Great Lakes area were also formed in the Paleozoic era. These are called fossil fuels and sometimes we can see the imprint of a fossil plant, such as a fern, on a lump of coal. Fossil fuels were formed from ancient plants.

Eventually these Paleozoic saltwater seas retreated and geological time passed: the Mesozoic Era, the Cenozoic Era. At the end of the Cenozoic Era, the Pleistocene Epoch or Ice Age began. The Great Lakes are creations of the Pleistocene.

What the Pleistocene Era or Great Ice Age Left Us

During the Great Ice Age or the Pleistocene era about a million or more years ago, about a quarter of Earth's land area became covered with ice in Europe, Greenland, Canada, and the United States. Increasing amounts of precipitation fell and were stored as snow. As a result, the sea levels dropped 300 to 400 feet resulting in a land bridge connecting Alaska and Asia.

Giant Bulldozers: the Work Of Glaciers

Snow began to accumulate, so much snow that the summer heat did not melt all of it. This went on year after year for thousands of years, until the snow in the Hudson Bay area of Canada grew so deep that it squeezed together, formed ice and then began to flow—something like pancake batter spreading out on a griddle except for the temperature: cold rather than hot. The glaciers grew and grew until some reached a height of seven miles. The weight of the ice was so great that it compressed the hard bedrock of the earth as easily as a child dents a balloon with one finger.

These moving mountains of ice called glaciers spread across the continent and then melted back north four times, something like a slow motion yo-yo. There were long periods of time in between glaciers when the weather became quite warm, but then another glacier would form and flow down from the north again. Each time the snow accumulated, then turned to ice and began to flow across mountains and valleys, great changes occurred in the soil, rocks, plant, and animal life.

Soil on top of the Canadian shield of hard bedrock was scraped off by the moving force of the glaciers, but the ancient rock of the Canadian Shield is so hard that the tremendous weight and power of moving ice could not crush it, but only rounded off mountains and left polished grooves in the hard rock. In other places, the glacier broke off huge boulders, froze them in their ice and carried them along slowly, then dropped them thousands of miles away.

The glaciers ground softer rocks into smaller and smaller pieces. The underside of the glacier picked up sharp pieces of stone and rasped them across the earth. The glacier rasped polished grooves in hard rock along Lake Superior's northern shore and other places such as Kelly's Island in Lake Erie.

Some Ice Age glaciers remain in northern Canada and Greenland. By studying these glaciers, geologists know that a glacier moves only 150 feet per day at the most. Sometimes it only moves a hundred or so feet per year. Although glaciers work slowly, they work powerfully. The last glacier went as far south as the Ohio River in the east and the Missouri River in the west.

These flowing mountains of ice dropped a blanket of sand, silt, and gravels of all sizes to a depth of 400 feet at its end and filled up river valleys from 1,000 to 1,500 feet on top of the bedrock surface. The glacier acted something like a conveyor belt dropping all sorts of debris off the end of the belt. We find deposits such as this today. These rocks, gravels, and sands can be of various sizes and types.

Sometimes a large chunk of ice imbedded in the soil would break off of the main glacier. This chunk of ice, when melted, became a lake or a pothole in the ground. There are many lakes of this type in the Great Lakes basin.

The Work of Melting Water From The Glaciers

When the glaciers finally melted for the last time, the water from the ice gushed across the land carving deep river beds. Flowing water sorts all kinds of material into layers according to their sizes and weights. The flowing melt water from the glaciers sorted the stones and soils into layers called stratifications. Today we find silt in layers; sand in layers; gravel in layers. This is the reason we find gravel pits with gravel of nearly all the same size; marshes with silt, and sand deposits. The sand dunes on the eastern edge of Lake Michigan are a gift of the glaciers and the west wind as the sand piled up along the shoreline.

Coastal lakes formed on the eastern shore of Lake Michigan: Muskegon Lake, Hamlin Lake and Silver Lake were caused 3,000 to 4,000 years ago by water levels 25 to 30 feet higher than they are today. The water flooded back into an area and then sandbars formed in rivers blocking their entrances to Lake Michigan. Currents moving along the shoreline as well as sand transported from inland closed the entrances of the rivers into Lake Michigan forming coastal lakes.

After the last major retreat of the ice sheet 14,000 years ago, glacial melt water ponded in the southernmost lake, Lake Erie. Then it ponded in the tip of Lake Michigan and parts of Lake Huron. By 10,500 years ago, major ice advances were over and the five Great Lakes were emerging, first at the southern ends and very gradually northward to Lake Superior. The glaciers melted over thousands of years. All five Great Lakes were free of ice about 3,000 years ago.

Free of the tremendous weight of the glaciers, the land slowly rebounded causing all five of the Great Lakes to begin draining out the St. Lawrence River. The Great Lakes' basins and the unique shapes of the land surrounding them emerged into the forms we now see: there is the mitten shape of Michigan's lower peninsula and some people think Lake Superior looks like the shape of a wolf's head with Isle Royale as the wolf's eye and Duluth, Minnesota the wolf's snout.

The shape of the land and the places where freshwater collected were determined by the action of Ice Age glaciers and later by the tremendous power of flowing water as the ice melted. The glaciers carved 35,000 islands in the Great Lakes.

Soon life invaded the glacial melt water from tributary rivers and streams such as the Mississippi and Ohio Rivers and the Ottawa and St. Lawrence Rivers. Microscopic one-celled plants and animals, larger plankton such as freshwater shrimp, freshwater worms, fingernail clams, and larvae of insects such as mayflies and caddis flies. Forage fishes such as lake herring, and emerald shiners and then predator fishes such as perch, lake whitefish, walleye, lake trout.

From glacial melt water devoid of life, unique ecosystems evolved in and around the Great Lakes.

Dynamic Great Lakes

The name for change is dynamic. Just as a young child changes from day to day, the geologically young Great Lakes change due to natural causes: shorelines erode as the levels of water rise and fall; marshes on the edges of the lakes change due to natural processes. Waves form peninsulas then wash them away; waves erase beaches then build them up again. Engineers have tried to counteract these powerful forces, but their efforts have usually been futile.

The shoreline along northern Lake Superior is still rising about an inch every one hundred years. The Earth is still rebounding from the tremendous pressure of the glaciers. Thousands of years ago this rebounding caused the system of lakes to flow toward the Atlantic.

All of the water flows from basin to basin beginning at the headwaters of Lake Superior in Canada's Lake Nipigon, down through a network of small streams and then downward still through the connecting channels between each of the Great Lakes and finally to the sea. Presently the Great Lakes have these elevations above sea level that causes them to flow from one to another constantly like water flowing from a series of basins.

Lake Superior is 600-feet/ 183 m above sea level
Lake Michigan and Lake Huron are both 581 feet/ 177m above sea level
Lake Erie is 571 feet/ 174 m above sea level
Lake Ontario is 264 feet/ 75 m above sea level
From Lake Ontario, the water flows down the St.
Lawrence River for 1,000 miles then mixes with the salt water of the Atlantic.

On the Great Lakes, linked by connecting rivers and man made locks, a ship may navigate for 2,342 miles from Duluth, Minnesota at the western tip of Lake Superior to Kingston, Ontario at the entrance of the St. Lawrence River and then down the Saint Lawrence River to the Gulf of St. Lawrence to the North Atlantic Ocean making shipping to and from the Great Lakes worldwide.

The Great Lakes hold 22.7 trillion cubic meters or 6 quadrillion gallons of fresh water. Half of the lakes' volume of water comes from precipitation. The rest of the water flowing into the lakes comes from tributaries draining into them and from groundwater. Rivers and streams around the Great Lakes basin drain an area of 194,000 square miles; twice the total surface area of the lakes. In comparison, other large lakes have drainage basins six times their size, therefore it is important for the integrity of the Great Lakes not to divert water out of the watershed.

The precipitation plus water flowing into the lakes from tributary streams and groundwater compensates for evaporation.

Lake Michigan water is diverted down the Mississippi River at Chicago that lowers the level of Lakes Michigan and Huron by 2.5 inches or 6 centimeters.

Locks built at the outlets of Lake Superior and Ontario affect the Lakes' levels. For example, the locks at Lake Ontario keep enough water flowing in the channels between the lakes for navigation and at the same time reduce Lake Ontario's fluctuations by one foot or .3 meters. A hydroelectric dam between Massena, New York and Cornwall, Ontario regulates water levels in Lake Ontario.

Water levels on the Great Lakes are extremely variable: fluctuations in the amount of rain and snow can affect water levels by ten feet.

In 1848, Louis Agassiz, a Swiss naturalist and professor of geology at Harvard had a hunch that immense sheets of ice once covered the world. To study the problem further, he mounted a scientific expedition to explore Lake Superior's northern shore along with his students and Ojibwa Indian guides. There he found boulders transported by the glacier and this supported his theory that the Great Lakes were carved out by glaciers and not caused by floods as people believed in the past.

In the Aftermath of the Last Glacier

Pure water does not occur in nature since water is a solvent. A solvent dissolves other substances. Rainwater dissolves some of the gases it passes through as it falls.

As water runs over rocks it picks up minerals such as iron or lime. Nourished by these minerals in the water, the first life to grow in fresh glacial melt water were phytoplankton: and then simple animals, protozoa or zooplankton that feed upon phytoplankton. Plankton such as desmids died and settled to the bottom to form a layer of muck.

Insects such as caddis flies that feed upon small organisms followed, then lake trout, herring, and whitefish had something to feed upon. These multiplied in the freshwater seas: the Great Lakes are geologically young and many ecological niches were available.

Every species lives in a niche where it makes its living and helps to check and balance populations of other species. The amount of space and food determines the carrying capacity of the environment: in other words, how many algae or fish or eagles can live in a certain place.

Paleo Indians as well as their descendants, the Native American tribes, prized the lake trout and whitefish they caught in nets and with hooks.

When European explorers first came to the Great Lakes shores 350 years ago, they found their waters produced fish they had never seen before in great quantities; most were ten pounds or over. The highest numbers of large fish were the primitive sturgeon: 200-300 pounds.

Great Lakes Sturgeon

There were five endemic species (fish found only in the Great Lakes). These fish had evolved over thousands of years since the glaciers' retreat and they belonged to the whitefish family, the salmon family as well as the blue pike and the Michigan grayling trout.

Oligotrophic, Mesotrophic and Eutrophic Lakes

Lake Superior's waters are the deepest, coldest and clearest of the Great Lakes. It is classified as an oligotrophic lake that means "little food."

Lake Huron and Lake Michigan are also oligotrophic in most of their area except for embayments or areas with man-made pollution. These three lakes are called the Upper Great Lakes and are younger than the lower Great Lakes since the glaciers melted back north over thousands and thousands of years therefore the northernmost lakes were the last to be free of ice.

The numbers of living things that can live in each lake and each bay within a lake can be measured by the amount of plankton its waters produce each year. The largest volume is phytoplanktors, the producers. More organisms can live in shallow sunlit water than in very deep parts of lakes. A bay of a large lake can be much more productive than out in the deep open waters.

Lake Erie is classified as eutrophic. Its waters are highly productive since it is a shallow lake surrounded by many wetlands. Eutrophic means "well fed." The plankton in eutrophic lakes constantly sinks to the bottom in a process called sedimentation.

Lake Ontario is classified as mesotrophic meaning in between oligotrophic and eutrophic, but 350 years ago, Lake Ontario was oligotrophic.

3

Lake Superior

"Go to the animals and they will teach you."
–Job 12:7

Elevation 600 ft 183 meters
Length 350 mi/563 km
Breadth 160 mi/259 km
Depth 489 ft/149 m average;
1,335 ft /407 m maximum
Volume 2,934 mi3 /12,230 km3
Water surface area 31,700 sq. mi 82,100 sq. km
Shoreline length 2,726 mi/ 4,385 km including islands
Elevation 600 ft / 183 m
Outlet St. Mary's River to Lake Huron
Retention replacement time 191 years
Population 474,150 U.S.
181,573 Canada

At 600 feet above sea level Lake Superior is the highest, northernmost, cleanest and coldest of the Great Lakes. In surface area, it is the largest freshwater lake in the world at 31,700 square miles. Superior could contain all of the other Great Lakes and three more Lake Eries. Its maximum depth is 1,335 feet; its average depth is 483 feet.

It would take about 190 years for the water to circulate through this greatest of the Great Lakes because the St. Mary's river channel connecting it with Lake Huron only allows a relatively small amount of water to flow out at one time.

Lake Superior is an Oligotrophic Lake

Lake Superior's cold water receives few nutrients, therefore it is called an oligotrophic lake (ill fed lake).

Its rocky shoreline lets fewer nutrients enter its waters, therefore there are fewer phytoplankton: zooplankton as well as fish are fewer and more far between than warmer, shallower and more nutrient rich lakes such as Lake Erie. Lake Michigan and Lake Huron are also classified as oligotrophic lakes. Cold-water species of plants and animals are adapted to these types of lakes.

Two Other Great Freshwater Lakes on Planet Earth

Lake Superior is the largest freshwater lake in the world in surface area: 31,700 square miles. Lake Baikal is slightly smaller in surface area, 31,699 square miles, but it is more than a mile deep making its volume greater: 5,500 cubic miles of water. This is equal to the volume of water in all the Great Lakes combined. Together, Lake Baikal and Lake Superior hold about 30 percent of fresh surface water; together Lake Baikal and all the Great Lakes hold about 40 percent of all the fresh surface water on Earth.

Unlike the relatively young Great Lakes, Lake Baikal is probably the world's oldest lake: 25 million years. Like Lake Superior, Lake Baikal was a pristine body of water with a unique ecosystem, but over the past twenty years, pulp and paper mills have degraded habitats and living things in both lakes.

Lake Victoria sprawls for 26,828 square miles across Africa's equator that makes it the third largest in surface area.

Lake Superior's Redfin Lake Trout

Let's take a look at one of Lake Superior's most desirable fish, the Isle Royale redfin lake trout to show how this fish lives its life cycle.

The deep waters of Lake Superior are still clean enough for this endemic species to reproduce.

A long and heavy female redfin lake trout slowly swims through the cool depths of Lake Superior; deep water is her habitat. Her deeply forked tail fans the water; her markings, a dapple of greens, grays and silver blend in with the colors of the rippling water. Her colors are her camouflage. She is ten years old, a prime age for breeding, and her belly bulges with eggs. Her instincts tell her it is time. The days have grown shorter and cooler in October; she feels an irresistible urge to return to the place where she was born: the rocks near Isle Royale. The memory of the place is imprinted within her body.

When she first reached maturity at the age of seven, she began the first of these journeys. Year after year, she returns to deposit her eggs so the next generation of lake trout may carry on their age old life cycles. Lake trout may live from thirteen to twenty years.

All around her, schools of the native Isle Royale redfin lake trout are milling about their birthplace, which is also their spawning place, as they have done for thousands of years. Lake trout, like their close relatives the salmon, are strong fish capable of traveling for hundreds of miles to their birthplace for spawning.

She waits until dark for the spawning to begin. The moon and stars shine on the surface of the calm lake. She is followed by a male lake trout who watches while hundreds of coral colored eggs cascade from her body onto the stony lake bottom. When she has finished laying her eggs, he positions himself over them and fertilizes them with a sticky, white substance called milt. The fertilized eggs fall into the deep crevices between the rocks where they will develop for the next four to five months. Not every egg will hatch though because many eggs are eaten by other fish such as suckers, yellow perch, minnows, and even other small lake trout.

This great abundance of life increases the possibility that the next generation will carry on the species in spite of the accidents that might cause the fertilized egg or the young fish to die, or be eaten.

During each breeding season, far more young fish are produced in any given body of water than that body of water can support. Predators are necessary to keep their numbers in check, otherwise the fish would starve or develop diseases.

From the rocky island nearby, the laughing cries of loons ring through the crisp autumn air. Loons, a species of diving waterfowl, live in northern lakes, and migrate south as days grow shorter. The spawning lake trout are safe from the sharp eyes of the bald eagle who has gone to roost until dawn.

Their spawning accomplished, the lake trout return to deeper water. They pass other native species of fish: whitefish and primitive looking bottom dwelling sturgeon—the largest of Great Lakes fish, and burbot, another bottom dwelling fish. They pass a nearly invisible commercial fishing net near the bottom which has caught a number of lake trout and by accident, a loon; some fish are dead and some struggle to free themselves from the fine mesh net that stretches for miles, catches fish by the gills, and eventually kills them.

The lake trout reaches the safety of deeper water where she will live through the winter. The Great Lakes never freeze all the way to the bottom in winter, even northernmost Lake Superior.

Native lake trout such as the redfins prefer depths of sixty to one hundred seventy five feet and they may swim for a hundred miles or more after spawning. Sailors must rely upon charts and a compass to find their way across Lake Superior. Lake trout use their instincts to guide them unerringly for hundreds of miles. Their senses, especially their senses of taste and smell and extra senses located in their lateral lines, lines that run along both sides of her body from the tail to the head, guide them to their traditional place for spawning. Beneath their lateral lines are a system of pores, canals and sense organs linked to the brain. With their lateral lines, fish are able to detect unseen enemies or prey. They sense currents, obstacles with the lateral line's sixth sense, in an intermediate area between hearing and touch; it allows the fish to remember low frequency vibrations and pressure waves built up as the fish passes rocks or other fish.

Experiments have shown that fish use their keen sense of smell to help them hone in on their traditional spawning grounds imprinted in their memories.

Great strength, speed and endurance make lake trout and their close relatives, the salmon, the champions of fish.

All summer the redfin lake trout feed upon freshwater sponges, crayfish, insects, and other fish such as the cisco, whitefish, smelt, perch, emerald shiners and long nose suckers and even feed upon ducklings or an occasional mouse that has fallen into the water. In winter, these fish must work harder to find food; they travel long distances in search of smaller fish to eat in winter.

For thousands of years, lake trout like this have lived in the deep-water habitats of Lake Superior, but now only a remnant population of the original species of lake trout remain.

In the springtime when young lake trout hatch from the egg, they carry a yolk sac on their belly that nourishes them in their first month of life. After the yolk sac has been absorbed into their bodies, they head for deeper water.

This is a precarious time for the young lake trout for everything from the great blue heron to seagulls to common loons; from walleye to perch to whitefish to smelt like to feed upon the young fry, but a few will grow up to repeat the life cycle as they have since the last glacier retreated and the lake trout migrated into the Great Lakes from southerly tributary streams where the fish had lived untouched by the ice during the Pleistocene, or Great Ice Age.

Native lake trout in Lake Superior indicate the water is still clean enough for the fry to survive. Lake trout in Lakes Michigan and Huron must be planted since these lakes have become too polluted for native lake trout to reproduce naturally.

Black fin Cisco

Black fin cisco, also called the chub, were plentiful in the depths of Lake Superior before 1897. When commercial fishermen discovered that they could haul in three tons in a single lift, which contained nothing but black fin cisco, they fished until they had nearly wiped out the whole species in ten years. Then it was no longer profitable for commercial fishermen to net black fin cisco because there were too few of them left.

Some people used to think that the Great Lakes were so large and the fish in them were so abundant that it wouldn't matter how many they caught or wasted. Today we know this is not true. It only took ten years for commercial fishermen to deplete the largest freshwater lake in the world of deepwater cisco.

Commercial Fisheries

In 1885, commercial fishermen caught 3,488,000 pounds of lake trout in Lake Superior; 6,431,000 pounds in Lake Michigan and 2,540 pounds in Lake Huron. But the catches of lake trout began to drop rapidly in Lake Huron around 1940, Lake Michigan around 1947, and Lake Superior during the 1950s.

There were two reasons for the drop in lake trout and whitefish populations: over fishing and the lamprey eel, a parasite which entered the Great Lakes from the Atlantic Ocean through navigation canals between Lake Erie and Lake Ontario.

In 1829 the first Welland Canal allowed shipping from the oceans to the Great Lakes and the lamprey eel slithered into four of the Great Lakes where it had never lived before.

Lamprey eels had been stopped by Niagara Falls until the shipping canal was built around it. By the 1930s the lamprey had begun to invade Lake Erie, Lake Huron and Lake Michigan. In fifteen years nearly all the whitefish and lake trout were gone from lakes Michigan, Huron, and Erie.

By the early 1950s the lampreys were navigating the Soo Locks or the St. Mary's River rapids, and soon half of Lake Superior's trout were destroyed.

Invasion by the parasitic lamprey eel was an unforeseen result of the canals that allowed ocean-going vessels to enter the Great Lakes. In saltwater seas predators keep lamprey eels in check, but in the Great Lakes where the lamprey had no natural enemies, they sucked the life out of native species, especially lake trout and whitefish.

This parasite destroys fish by attaching itself to the fish's side with its large suction cup like mouth. It then drains the life out of the fish it feeds upon. This wounds, and may kill the fish. During its adult life, which lasts eighteen months, each sea lamprey can kill forty or more pounds of fish. A lake trout or whitefish with a lamprey attached to it becomes weak as the sea lamprey grows strong: the lamprey may reach the length of a foot and a half by sucking the life out of the fish.

In 1962 the U. S. Fish and Wildlife Service developed a chemical, TFM (3-trifluormethyl-4-nitrophenol) that would kill young lamprey. Unlike DDT that is harmful to the ecosystem, TFM proved to be harmless to everything but the lamprey larvae it was intended to kill. Since the lamprey eels migrate in spring and early summer to tributary streams where spawning occurs, TFM could be applied to the areas of small streams where lampreys spawn to kill their larvae.

Adult sea lampreys die after spawning. The lampricide, TFM has been effective in getting rid of the larvae in small streams, but in the St. Mary's River with its powerful current, the results have been less successful. Sterilizing and releasing male lamprey eels in the St. Mary's River may be a solution. The lamprey continues to breed so TFM must be applied each year. Since the currents in the St. Mary's River are so powerful, it is difficult to keep lampreys controlled. Granular Bayluscide suited to the deep parts of the St. Mary's River is applied with helicopters, and there is a lamprey trapping program underway. With these programs, sturgeon, burbot, lake trout and salmon have a fighting chance to survive.

The Largest Fish in the Great Lakes

The largest and most primitive fish in the Great Lakes is the sturgeon. Cruising along on bottoms of the lakes, they remind us of dinosaurs that roamed planet Earth in earlier epochs. Their huge bodies are supported by cartilage as well as bone. They can weigh up to 300 pounds, and like some dinosaurs, they have rows of plates along their heads and bodies to protect them. When all of the lakes and their tributary rivers were cleaner than they are now, and when there were no dams to block their way, these great fish would spawn by running up rivers. In Lake Superior, they still run up the Sturgeon River in Michigan's Upper Peninsula to spawn and may be seen surfacing like submarines, sticking their snouts above the water in pools below waterfalls. The sturgeon has been living in the Great Lakes ever since the last glaciers retreated and fish entered the lakes through crystal clear tributary streams. Sturgeon's eggs (roe) are a delicacy known as caviar when processed for human food.

In 1974 the sturgeon was included on a list of threatened species. These ancient fish cruise the lake bottom feeding upon crayfish, insect larvae, clams and bottom plants. This is their ecological niche where they use their long shovel shaped snout with a sucker-like mouth underneath to feed. Two whisker-like barbels near their mouths help them to feel their way along the bottom. Sturgeon are slow to mature; they may not spawn until 14 to 22 years.

Sturgeon decreased further in the 1920s when dams were built on rivers blocking their traditional spawning places and slowing down the flow of rivers.

Bottom Habitats

Lake bottoms are catch basins that collect soil that has washed into them from shore. Rocks, clay and fine silt are sorted by waves that carry the finer particles out into the deep water; coarser sediments settle near the shore. Bottom sediments support beneficial bacteria that recycle dead material, plankton, the larval stages of insects and bottom dwelling fish such as the sturgeon and the burbot. In the gray black ooze of the bottom, the burbot, a cold water species of fish lies nearly concealed by its brown and black markings like a tortoise shell comb, a fish that has been increasing its numbers in the Great Lakes. The burbot has been found in deep water niches (as deep as 700 feet) where they grow stout as they compete with lake trout for food. They satisfy their voracious appetites upon other deepwater fish such as the whitefish. Because over fishing, pollution, and the lamprey eel lowered the numbers of fish in the Great Lakes, the Departments of Natural Resources in the United States and Canada have experimented with planted fish in all of the Great Lakes.

Pink Salmon

Pink salmon, a relative of the lake trout, are from the saltwater Pacific Ocean. Some of these fish were accidentally washed down the drain at an experiment station on Lake Superior in 1955 and to everyone's surprise, the fish returned to the drain two years later to spawn. They established themselves in the cold freshwater of Lake Superior then reached Lake Michigan and Lake Huron via the St.

Mary's River, which is a freeway for fish. Pink salmon weigh from three to five pounds at maturity and sometimes reach ten pounds. The adult male develops a large hump on his back and a hooked snout. On the northeast side of Lake Huron, the spawning streams of Georgian Bay are filled with pink salmon during their spawning time. Some people do not like non-native species in the Great Lakes because they use the same places to feed and spawn (the same ecological niche) used by native species, such as the brook trout, and may crowd them out.

Hybrid Salmon: Pinook

Pink salmon, a type of Pacific salmon, were accidentally introduced into Lake Superior in the mid 1950s in the Thunder Bay, Ontario area according to Dr. R. Greil, and spread into Lakes Huron and Michigan. There they encountered another planted fish, the Chinook salmon. In the 1990s the first hybrids, the crossing of pink and Chinook salmon, occurred in the St. Mary's River. This was the only place in the world where there is documentation on hybridization of these salmon. The fish were tested for DNA at the University of Michigan. All of the hybrids tested indicate that the crossing was done by female Chinooks and male pink salmon. All Pacific salmon die after spawning since they are a two year fish, but some in Lake Superior will live for three years. This hybrid fish, the pinook, does not die after spawning. In the dynamic Great Lakes, changes continue to occur, surprising fishermen and scientists alike.

Niches

Some fish that live in deep water are the primitive sturgeon and burbot, as well as cisco, native whitefish, redfin lake trout, Lake Superior siscowet, or fat lake trout.

Planted fish such as the Atlantic and pink salmon, brown trout, Chinook salmon, coho salmon, cruise the open waters while the shallower, warmer, more nutrient rich embayments harbor native small mouth bass, walleye, northern pike, yellow perch, and suckers.

Every species has a niche in the environment where it earns its living.

The energy of the sun moves through phytoplankton, zooplankton and fish from the top layer of the water to the depths with various species producing or consuming or recycling. Energy moves through every part of the lake when the ecosystem is working well.

Limnologists (scientists who study fresh water) discovered that 48 percent of the producers (phytoplankton) in Lake Superior are an extremely small species called pico plankton. These minuscule producers could not be collected in ordinary plankton nets, but had to be filtered out of the water with membrane filters and then examined through an electron microscope. Phytoplankton such as these multiply rapidly on sunny days, replenishing the base of the food pyramid. They are grazed by zooplankton; the zooplankton are devoured by small fish, and small fish by larger fish. The sun's energy moves through the food pyramid moving energy from the top layers of the water column to the bottom.

The interconnected communities of plants, insects, crustaceans, fish, birds and mammals each have a niche; that is, its own place and way of making its living in the community with each species adapted to the other as well as to the conditions and seasonal changes in each body of water.

Highly diversified communities of plants and animals had evolved in the Great Lakes for several thousand years and in a complex manner, everything was connected to everything else. We do not know for sure exactly how many species of fish lived in the Great Lakes before the time people began to exploit the land and water for lumbering, farming and fishing, but it is estimated that there were between 125 and 180 species. Today there are fewer than half of the native species of fish that lived in the Great Lakes before the European immigrants began to exploit them. Other species have been greatly reduced.

41

In the last two decades, fish biologists have introduced new species of fish to the Great Lakes, but these are still experimental.

Some Native Fish in Lake Superior

Redfin lake trout, siscowet (fat lake trout) whitefish, brook trout, small mouth bass, sturgeon, walleye, yellow perch, northern pike, burbot, black fin cisco (extinct)

Introduced or accidental: Atlantic salmon, brown trout, Chinook salmon, smelt, pink salmon, ruffe, lamprey eel, alewife, pinook (a new hybrid) what about steelhead?

4

Lake Michigan and Lake Huron: Siamese Twins

"If there is magic on this planet, it is contained in water."
–Loren Eiseley

Lake Michigan

Elevation: 581 ft. 176 metres
Length: 307 mi 494 km
Breadth: 118 miles 190 kilometres
Average depth: 279 ft. 85 metres
Maximum depth: 925 ft. 282 metres
Volume 1,180 cu mi 4,920 cu km
Water area 22,300 sq mi 57, 750 sq km
Retention time: 99 years
Population: U. S. 10,057,026
Outlet: Straits of Mackinac to Lake Huron

In some ways, Lake Huron and Lake Michigan are like Siamese

twins: hooked together at the Straits of Mackinac, they are the same sea level, 577 ft., and about the same area (Lake Michigan is slightly smaller in surface area but holds a greater volume of water due to its greater depth). Lake Michigan has its outlet through the Straits of Mackinac into Lake Huron and also through the Chicago River that was reversed to protect the city's drinking water supply from viruses and bacteria after cholera and typhoid outbreaks in the 1800s. Chicago's wastewater is diverted down a man made canal to the Illinois and Mississippi River systems rather than into Lake Michigan. Since Chicago is the most populous city on the Great Lakes, this diversion is good for the health of Lake Michigan as well as the people of Chicago. The southern end of the lake is a cul-de-sac where there is not much circulation causing pollutants to collect. Lake Michigan looks like an elongated water balloon with water bulging at its bottom and a narrow outlet at the top. Pollutants caught in the bottom of the balloon where there is little circulation take an estimated 99 years to circulate out through the straits of Mackinaw.

Major industrial centers such as Milwaukee, Wisconsin, Chicago, Illinois, and Gary, Indiana with large cities, large-scale agriculture, and shipping add to the burden of pollution in lower Lake Michigan.

Lake Michigan's Door Peninsula in Wisconsin and Lake Huron's Bruce Peninsula in Ontario, Canada are mirror image twins. These fingers of land, formed of layers of limestone/dolomite, are part of the Niagara Escarpment, laid down from the fossil remains of sea creatures from ancient salt seas.

Reefs left behind by prehistoric corals in ancient salt seas lie not far below the surface. These reefs have always caused shipwrecks on the Great Lakes. So many sailors have been lost on the Great Lakes that an 1,850 pound solid marble crucifix was placed 70 feet underwater in Little Traverse Bay in Lake Michigan, near Petoskey to commemorate them. Many of these shipwrecks occurred in the 1880s to early 1900s when ships had wooden rather than steel hulls and were not guided by modern navigational aids. The wooden timbers of these ships that once carried lumber, iron ore, and passengers are well preserved in the cold waters of the lake bottoms. Silvery whitefish dodge in and out of the shipwrecks' timbers in pursuit of alewives. Sometimes scuba divers investigate the wrecks.

Lake Huron

Elevation: 581(the same as Lake Michigan) 176 metres
Length: 206 mi. 331 km
Breadth: 245 km.
Depth 194 ft 59 m average 748 ft. 229 m maximum
Volume 849 cu mi. 3,540 cu km
Retention time 22 years
Outlet: St. Clair River
Population: 1,502,687 U.S. 1,191,467 Canada

Lake Huron is 23,000 square miles, which makes it the second largest Great Lake in area. It is the third deepest Great Lake with a maximum depth of 750 feet. Lake Huron contains 15% (849 cubic miles of the water) in the Great Lakes and has a flushing time of 22 years. Although the water quality is oligotrophic in the upper parts of the lake, Saginaw Bay in Lake Huron and Green Bay in Lake Michigan are eutrophic and polluted with wastes from farming, lumbering and manufacturing.

On the Canadian side of Lake Huron, Georgian Bay was mistakenly called a sixth Great Lake by early explorers since it is nearly separated from the rest of Lake Huron by Manitoulan Island and the Bruce Peninsula. Manitoulin Island, (1,068 square miles) is the largest freshwater island in the world and Georgian Bay is the largest bay on the Great Lakes.

Mayflies Are Indicators of a Healthy Environment

The food chains in these two lakes have changed rapidly in the past 100 years. In the wetlands and in embayments of numerous islands of Lake Michigan and Lake Huron, mayflies are good indicators of a healthy habitat. Some people call them fish flies; there are several varieties well known by fishermen who tie artificial flies.

On a warm day in late June or early July, the northern waters of the Lakes Huron and Michigan and all of Lake Superior undulate gently. Reflections of trees shine in their glassy waters. Suddenly the surface pops with the emerging of billions of fish flies wiggling free from their cases; they are lucky if they live to fly off before a fish sucks them out of the water first. If they fly, ducklings, songbirds and flocks of seagulls gobble them like guests at a festive banquet.

The graceful flies with soft bodies and transparent veined wings that do survive, find a mate, mate, and then the female lays about 3,000 eggs on the surface of the water. The eggs sink to the bottom, develop into larvae, or the nymph stage. On the bottom they stay for one or two years, feeding upon plankton and molting up to 30 times until it is time for them to emerge as adult insects, popping out of their casings like popcorn. The life cycles begin again. There are many varieties of fish flies and their presence shows that the food chain is healthy.

When water becomes too polluted, desirable types of insects disappear. Fifty years ago, Saginaw Bay's waters became depleted of oxygen because of too much pollution; as a result, the mayflies disappeared.

Great Changes in the Lakes

In their oligotrophic waters, cold water species of fish such as the native lake trout and whitefish thrived until they were over-fished by commercial fishermen from the 1880s on; lamprey eels destroyed most of their remnant populations.

With very few large predator fish to devour them, another invader from the sea, the alewife, exploded in population. The lakes' ecological balance was destroyed.

Freshwater fishes are of three kinds: those which must live in fresh water all of the time; those that spend most of their time in fresh water and some time in salt water, and those that migrate between fresh and salt water spending about equal time in each. Some fish such as the alewife that lived in saltwater have adapted to the Great Lakes' fresh water, but changes in temperature can cause die offs.

The Alewife, a Misfit from the Sea

Over fishing and the lamprey eel upset the ecological balance. With few large predator fish such as the native lake trout and whitefish to keep their numbers in check, an unwanted small bony fish, the alewife, became a major problem in Lake Michigan and Lake Huron.

The alewife entered the interconnected lakes and their tributaries from the Atlantic Ocean when the Welland Canal opened up the Great Lakes to international shipping. Like the lamprey eel, this saltwater fish was a misfit in the Great Lakes ecosystems.

In 1954, alewives were caught for the first time in Lake Michigan. In the early 1960s, the total number of living things in Lake Michigan was over 90% alewives. They washed up on beaches and died in great numbers—fifty percent of the alewife population died in 1967. Tons of dead alewives washed up on Lake Michigan beaches attracting flies which laid eggs on the dead fish. The beaches were soon crawling with maggots; the stench of rotting fish, and clouds of flies made the beaches unbearable.

The great population of alewife devoured populations of large zooplankton such as freshwater shrimp, upon which other types of fish such as perch relied for their food supply. Perch became scarce.

Coho Salmon Planted in Tributaries of Lake Superior and Lake Michigan A Success: Salmon Planted in All Great Lakes

Because the native lake trout and whitefish had become scarce due to over fishing and the lamprey eel, alewife populations exploded. There were not enough predator fish to keep their numbers in check. Tons of dead alewives washed up on the beaches.

In 1966 a biologist, Dr. Howard Tanner, came up with a creative solution to the alewife problem: plant coho salmon to feed upon the pesky little alewives. Three quarters of a million small coho salmon were stocked in the tributaries of Lake Superior and Lake Michigan where they had never lived before. Coho, or silver salmon, a type of Pacific salmon, grew rapidly in the Great Lakes with the huge supply of alewives to feed upon. By 1967 people began catching coho with rods and reels.

The planted coho grew so well that the Michigan Department of Natural Resources planted the largest strain of Pacific salmon in 1967, the Chinook or king salmon in Lakes Michigan and Huron.

Now four to six inch salmon are planted yearly in tributary streams. Hungry seagulls, ducks, water snakes, frogs, catfish, walleye and northern pike snatch the planted fish, but if they escape the teeth and bills of their predators, they grow heavy and strong on a diet of insects and zooplankton, then forage fish such as alewife, smelt, emerald shiners (minnows) and then larger fish.

Other Planted Fish

Coho and Chinook salmon were not the first fish to be planted in the Great Lakes. Lake Michigan has received other non-native species that take over the niches of native species.

Carp

Carp, a bottom dwelling fish that can tolerate warm water and pollution were planted as a food fish by European immigrants. Today carp are considered a nuisance because they uproot plants and destroy the habitat for native fish such as perch wherever they are.

Smelt

Like salmon, carp, and alewives, smelt are not native species. The smelt, a small silvery ocean fish, was introduced into a tributary connected to Lake Michigan in 1912. By 1930, the smelt had spread to all the Great Lakes.

Once in the Great Lakes, their population exploded. They competed with the native lake herring because they filled the same ecological niche. With two fish competing for the same food, the lake herring's numbers fell to one third its former numbers.

In April or May, smelt swim up streams at night to spawn when the waters are cool and dark. When the smelt are running, people scoop them up in nets and carry them home by the bucketful. They make tasty meals.

Smelt are also delightful morsels to trout and salmon. They never grow very large, 6-10 inches, and many other fish feed on them, yet some smelt always survive because they are not easy for larger fish to see. They, like many other species, have what is called protective coloration. Their greenish back blends in with the dark water below so a predator fish looking down cannot easily spot it. Their silvery belly blends in with the sunlit water above when a predator looks up.

Brown Trout

Brown trout were imported from Germany and released into Michigan's Pere Marquette River, a tributary to Lake Michigan, in 1884. Some of these fish, the lake run brown trout, a close relative of the Atlantic salmon spend part of their lives in the big lake.

Rainbow Trout or Steelhead   non native

The native rainbow trout also planted in tributary streams grew large in the Great Lakes. A large strain of rainbow trout called the steelhead lives in the lakes and spawns in tributary streams.

Of the non-native fish, the Chinook or king salmon is the largest; typically they weigh from 20 to 30 pounds. The coho or silver salmon, lake run brown trout, and steelhead trout average about eight pounds and may reach 30 pounds.

Return of the Native Lake Trout

With the alewife problem solved, hatchery-raised lake trout were planted in upper Lake Michigan and Lake Huron and then later on reefs known by commercial fishermen who fished the Great Lakes many years ago. These reef formations were built by ancient corals that lived when the area was covered by ancient saltwater seas, millennia before the Great Lakes were formed by the fresh melt water of glaciers. Deep-water coral reefs make an ideal place for the fish to lay their eggs since there are crevices for the developing eggs to fall into, and the water is cleaner and more protected from predators than at the mouths of rivers.

In the fall, anadromous fish (the coho and Chinook and pink salmon) gather at the mouths of the stream where they were planted to prepare for their swim upstream. At two or three years of age, four

50

years for Chinook, they are ready to spawn. Unlike the lake trout that lives for thirteen to twenty years, these salmon die after they have spawned. The natural life cycle of anadromous fish is to hatch in a stream, return to the sea (or a lake), eat voraciously and grow to a large size, and then return to spawn in the river where they were planted or hatched. Like lake trout, they have the ability to imprint the place where they hatched through their keen senses of taste and smell; they are both superior species, strong fish that can swim great distances.

Unlike lake trout that lay their eggs on lake rocks and reefs, salmon and steelhead leap through waterfalls to reach their destination upstream. Where dams interfere, sometimes engineers build a fish ladder for the salmon to leap up on, to get around the dam. On the Grand River in Michigan, there are fish ladders in Grand Rapids and Lansing. In Grand Rapids, seven small ledges on the west bank of the river allows people to view the large fish ascending in September through October. After spawning, salmon die within a couple of weeks, an easy meal for raccoons, bears, mink, opossums, owls, hawks and eagles, as well as other fish and plankton.

Splake

By the 1980s, every state and province surrounding the Great Lakes had planted exotic species of fish. Ontario and Michigan experimented with the splake, a hybrid of the native lake trout and brook (or speckled) trout. The splake is not able to reproduce because it is a hybrid. However, none of the planted fish have been able to reproduce on their own in great enough numbers for sports fishers who want to catch them, so hatchery-raised fish are stocked year after year in Lake Michigan and Lake Huron as well as Lake Erie and Lake Ontario. In contrast, research showed that 90% of the coho salmon caught in Lake Superior and its tributary streams were from natural reproduction by 1990. The original species of lake trout still reproduce naturally.

Indicators of a Clean or Polluted Habitat

The types of fish that can survive in a habitat indicate how healthy it is. In some Michigan, Wisconsin, Illinois, and Indiana streams, pollution tolerant carp do well, but salmon eggs will not hatch because the streams are too muddy and silt laden and do not have a high enough level of dissolved oxygen. Salmon eggs can only hatch in clear, gravel-bottomed streambeds with a high level (7 ppm) of dissolved oxygen.

Clear, cold, swiftly running water picks up oxygen from the air as it flows. Cold water can retain more oxygen than warm water. These high quality streams are not often found in places highly populated by human beings. Because most eggs do not hatch naturally, hatchery reared salmon are placed in tributary streams every year to replace the previous generations. The money paid by sports fishers to buy fishing licenses finance the fish-stocking program.

With trout and salmon keeping the numbers of alewife in check, the ecosystem became healthier. Populations of zooplankton increased and then, with their food supply once again abundant, native species such as perch, chubs, and lake trout, and lake run rainbow trout, called steelhead, increased.

The bloater chub, a type of whitefish native to the Great Lakes were nearly extinct, but have now recovered in great numbers.

Nature is flexible and resilient. In the Great Lakes our interference taught us quite a few life and death lessons as populations of living things have been exploited, nearly wiped out by accidentally introduced species and experimented with.

The changes brought about in the last 100 years have been profound in Lake Michigan and Lake Huron. The lakes original interconnected ecosystems of native species such as lake trout and whitefish prior to the 1850s changed to an unhealthy environment dominated by exotic species such as the lamprey eel and alewife 100 years later. Today Lake Michigan and Huron have improved.

When pollution laws went into effect in the 1970s, all living things benefitted: native as well as planted fish such as coho, Chinook and lake trout. When these planted fish began to die off in the 1990s, we knew that all is still not well in the lakes. Toxic wastes are still a major concern.

Dioxins and PCBs linger in the Great Lakes, in bottom sediments and food pyramids. The long-lived lake trout accumulate them and their newly hatched fry die in a few days. Dr. Richard E. Peterson with Philip M. Cook believe that dioxins and related chemicals are the likely cause. They have researched the problem for twenty years.

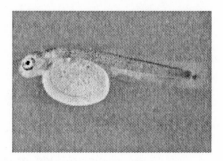

Lake trout with yolk sac

According to Barry Commoner, the majority of dioxins reach the Great Lakes through the incineration of municipal and hospital wastes around the Great Lakes. Some dioxins ride airstreams and reach the Great Lakes from as far away as Florida and Texas. Incompletely burned wastes are carried to the great surface area of the Great Lakes through the air.

PCBs (polychlorinated biphenyls) are a group of 209 long-lived chemicals tied to cancer of the brain, liver, skin and breast. They have caused developmental problems in children.

Fish Found in Lake Michigan and Huron

Through the connecting St. Mary's River and the Straits of Mackinac, strong superior species such as trout and salmon swim from Lake Superior and Lake Michigan to Lake Huron and back again.

Planted trout and salmon may face many hazards: modern gill nets set by Native Americans who are allowed to use them; commercial fisheries in Wisconsin, Michigan and Illinois; and harmful chemicals which are the byproducts of manufacturing processes and incinerators.

Some Native Fish

Sturgeon, northern pike, small mouth bass, whitefish, chubs, lake trout, yellow perch, burbot, sucker, American eel, lake herring, menominee, rainbow trout (steelhead).

non native

Introduced or Accidental Fish

Chinook salmon, coho salmon, pink salmon, brown trout, splake (hybrid), Atlantic salmon, ruffe, alewife, lamprey eel, right eyed flounder, smelt, nine spine stickleback, pinook (hybrid), carp.

5

Lake Erie

"This country is so temperate, so fertile, and so beautiful, that it may justly be called the earthly paradise of North America."
–Antoine de la Mothe Cadillac, 1702

Lake Erie Dimensions

Length 241 mi/338 km
Breadth 57 mi/92 km
Depth 62 ft/ 19 m average
210 ft/ 64 m maximum
Volume ll6 cu mi/483 cu km
Water Surface Area 9,906 sq mi
25,657 sq km
Drainage Basin Area 22,720 sq mi
58,800 sq km
Shoreline Length 871 mi/l,400 km
including islands
Elevation 571 ft/ 174 m
Retention Replacement Time 2.6 years (shortest of the lakes)
Population 10,017,530 (U.S.) l,664,6397(Canada)
Outlet: Niagara River and Welland Canal

In surface area, Lake Erie is the fourth largest of the Great Lakes: 9,906 square miles (25,657 sq km) and the twelfth largest in the world. In volume it is 116 cubic miles (483 cu km), the smallest in water volume of the Great Lakes. It lies further south than the other Great Lakes, therefore its climate is warmer: it was the first Great Lake to be completely emerged when the last glacier began its slow retreat northward some 12,000 years ago.

Because it is the shallowest of the five Great Lakes, (its average depth is 62 ft (19 m)), it is sometimes treacherous for boaters because of sudden squalls that whip the water.

Erie is classified as a eutrophic (well fed) lake because of the nutrients entering it, resulting in high numbers of plankton, and fish.

Lake Erie's Ecosystem

A great blue heron wades along a coastal wetland and suddenly captures a frog in his long beak. When a boater approaches the long-legged heron too closely, it suddenly rises gracefully into the air and with its loud clattering voice, warns the other herons of an intruder. In the shallow water, a large school of perch swim around a pile of stones.

Near the shore, a family of beavers has built a den out of tree branches they have cut with their sharp, chisel-like teeth. The marsh teems with young fish, reptiles, and small mammals. For the great blue heron, it is a delicatessen stocked with all of his favorite foods. Marshes and coastal wetlands are important as breeding places for many types of plankton, crayfish, fish and birds, for mammals such as the muskrat and beaver, and for water loving animals such as frogs, snakes, and turtles. Many types of birds nest and feed in wetlands and during the spring time especially, fill the air with their sounds: ducks, herons, ospreys, and many types of smaller birds such as the redwing blackbird and yellow warbler. The sparrow hawk or kestrel lives in wetland areas.

Wetlands produce more wildlife and plants than any other type of Great Lakes habitat. Since wetlands are so important to the environment, laws have been passed to prevent people from filling in what they might mistakenly believe are useless areas. So far the Great Lakes region has lost as much as two-thirds of its original wetlands. Blessed with lush coastal wetlands, Lake Erie supports both large human and wildlife populations.

Lake St. Clair's Fresh Water Delta, The Largest in the World

Lake Huron's clear turquoise color waters flow from its southernmost tip, down through a seven mile channel, the St. Clair River, then into hundreds of channels that make up the world's largest freshwater delta to heart-shaped Lake St. Clair, which has its outlet at the point of the heart into the Detroit River. The combined waters from the Upper Great Lakes, Superior, Michigan and Huron, flow downward into Lake Erie. Migratory birds such as the canvasback and redhead ducks and about 50 percent of North America's whistling swans use Lake St. Clair and its wetlands as a stopover on their migrations. Mayflies hatch in such great numbers that people living along Lake St. Clair must hose the dead flies off of their cars and houses.

In the Detroit River, the National Wildlife Refuge on Grassy Island provides habitat for migrating birds in the fall and spring, even though it is close to heavily industrialized areas on both the Canadian and U. S side.

The Detroit River's strong current moves the jade green water swiftly into Lake Erie.

The marshes along the St. Clair River and its delta, Lake St. Clair, and the Detroit River are ninety miles of productive habitat for wildlife between Lake Huron and Lake Erie. This is considered part of the Lake Erie ecosystem.

Marshes: Nature's Sponge and Water Filter

Wetlands are essential to all of the Great Lakes ecosystems. The reason is they soak up excess runoff water like giant sponges, and they reduce flooding and erosion; they filter out pollutants; they help recharge underground water supplies, and they are nurseries for fish, birds, reptiles, and insects.

Marshes have standing water from less than an inch to several feet deep. Cattails, sedges, rushes arrowhead, and other soft stemmed plants have their roots and part of the stems under water and their top parts above water. These plants specialize in filtering out pollutants and breaking them down into less harmful substances. They also trap nutrients in their roots, stems, and leaves and provide carbon, oxygen, and other elements that enrich bodies of water where they stand. For this reason, they support communities of plankton, fish, birds, and mammals. It's easy to see how valuable marshes are.

Coastal wetlands are found between open water and the land rising up from the shoreline. Coastal wetlands of the Great Lakes differ from other wetlands since they are always renewing themselves. Since water levels on the Great Lakes are always changing, they do not fill up with heavy vegetation like wetland areas inland such as bogs, marshes, and wet meadows. Coastal wetlands expand inland when the water level is low and move again when the water level is high.

If natural processes are allowed to work without too much human interference, the ecosystem is self-regulating. In the past, many wetlands were drained to make more dry land, yet wetlands are valuable as they are.

Lake Erie's Wetlands

Only twenty-five miles from downtown Detroit, people with binoculars watch the spring migration of raptors: various species of hawks at Point Mouille State Game Area, a wetland known for its wildlife. Wild rice grows here; muskrats and raccoons find the marsh a good habitat.

Another famous wetland is Point Pelee National Park on the Canadian side of Lake Erie, 51 miles from Windsor, Ontario. During spring and fall, more than 70 varieties of migrating birds use Point Pelee's 2,500 acres of marshland and sand dunes as a stopover on a major flyway for bird migrations.

200 Endangered Plants on the Great Lakes

Along the shorelines of Lake St. Clair, the western edge of Lake Erie, as well as Lake Huron's Saginaw Bay, the prairie white fringed orchids nod their clusters of white flowers in the breeze. Once common, these orchids are now an endangered species. Of over 2,000 plant species around the Great Lakes, more than 200 are threatened or endangered due to a loss of habitat. Plants are an important part of the Great Lakes' ecology. Their roots hold the soil in place that otherwise would be washed or blown away. They enrich the soil, add to the beauty of the landscape, and the plant communities along the shores of the Great Lakes are distinct from all others on Earth.

Imagine what the explorer Cadillac saw when he first viewed Lake Erie: great woodlands surrounded it, tributary rivers ran clear, and wildflowers grew in profusion. He called it an earthly paradise.

Three hundred years later, the Lake Erie shoreline and waters still have a temperate climate and a productive ecosystem, although not quite the paradise the explorer Cadillac saw. Lake Erie has been profoundly changed in the past 150 to 200 years.

During the 1700s and 1800s, white settlers in the Lake Erie watershed cut the woodlands, and burned prairies to convert it to farmland. In the process, the roots that held valuable topsoil in place disappeared and the soil washed into tributaries and the lake. They built dams on the rivers for mills, slowing the flow and preventing fish such as the sturgeon from going upstream to spawn.

Then, just as today, they drained and filled marshlands; industries and cities dumped their wastes into the lake and its tributaries. As human populations grew and their life styles changed from the horse and buggy to the automobile, the wastes both changed and increased. Because people have used the shores of this area for building, little of the original habitats remain.

Lake Erie's Fish

Commercial fishing with seine nets and pollution changed Lake Erie's ecosystem completely. In the 1800s and early 1900s, cisco were common, especially in Lake Erie; their numbers declined after the 1920s because the fish was sensitive to pollution and it was over-fished.

Northern pike, lake herring, lake whitefish, and sauger were recorded by commercial fishermen between the late 1800s and 1950. One by one whole communities of fish became so scarce no one fished for them any more.

As bad as things were, Lake Erie's problems became even worse in the 1950s. As the population and industrial production increased over the years, the lake became overloaded with nutrients from wastewater plants and industries. These nutrients, especially phosphates, caused the water to become choked with too much algae which died, sank to the bottom, and nourished new algae blooms. The decaying algae depleted the water of dissolved oxygen.

The Cleveland Waterworks made a daily count of the number of algal cells found in one millimeter of Lake Erie water taken at the point of the city's water supply intake in the lake since 1919. In 1927 the annual average count was about 100 algae per milliliter; in 1945 the count had increased to 800; in 1964 it reached 2,500. In the western basin of Lake Erie, a number of careful bottom surveys between 1929 and 1953 had shown that mayfly nymphs were the most common lake bottom species. But a change took place in 1953.

An ecologist, Dr. N. W. Britt from the Institute of Hydrobiology at Ohio State University, found that the mayfly nymphs he collected had died due to low oxygen content in the water. Dr. Britt recorded a turning point in the ecology of Lake Erie. For the first time in its 12,000 year history, Lake Erie did not have enough oxygen to support an important part of its food pyramid. This was due to an overloading of organic wastes from municipal sewage plants around the lake. These made the algae bloom until the lake had the consistency of pea soup. The algae grew quickly and died quickly sinking to the lake bottom, fouling the water with its decay.

Taken over by primitive blue green algae, the whole food chain collapsed. Populations of lake whitefish, sauger and blue pike disappeared completely in the 1950s. Even bottom dwelling burbot and suckers became scarce.

The Democratic Process

Citizens were dismayed with the degraded condition of Lake Erie. In many places they were warned not to fish or swim because of pollution. Then a dramatic event captured the nation's attention: In July of 1969, Ohio's most polluted river became so coated with oil and debris that the river caught fire in Cleveland's factory area. The load of pollution from meat-rendering plants, steel mills, chemical plants, and inadequately treated sewage along with runoff from fertilized fields further upstream on the Cuyahoga River did not capture our attention in the same way. It took a river on fire for people to really get concerned about the Cuyahoga as well as other tributary rivers in the Lake Erie basin with their load of pollutants. Through the democratic process, the people demanded a solution, and were willing to pay for it through taxes.

The Federal Water Quality Administration launched a one and a half billion dollar municipal sewage treatment program for the Erie

Basin which included the five surrounding states: Michigan, Ohio, New York, Pennsylvania, and Indiana.

There are still occasional beach closings around the Great Lakes due to heavy loads of coliform bacteria from cities and farms.

Manufacturers of detergents helped tremendously by removing the phosphates from their products that were adding to algae bloom problems all over the country. After phosphates were removed from detergents by the manufacturers, the Detroit River showed a 70 percent improvement. Even though Lake Erie was nearly polluted to the stage of no return, its recovery was more rapid than people had expected. It has an advantage the other four Great Lakes do not have—water flushes out of it rapidly: the drop between Lake Erie and Lake Ontario is 307 feet (99 metres) down the Niagara River and then takes a spectacular plunge over Niagara Falls. Because of this, it takes Lake Erie only 2.6 years for its water to be completely exchanged compared to 191 years for water to flush out of the narrow outlet of Lake Superior.

The clean up paid off. With cleaner waters, the no swimming and no fishing signs were removed and people began to enjoy Lake Erie again. The mayflies have returned and by 1999 made a strong comeback in Lake Erie.

Lake Erie's Dramatic Recovery

Today Lake Erie no longer looks like a dead or dying body of water. It has become famous as a sports fishing hotspot for walleye, drum, and perch, fish well adapted to warm water. Cold-water species such as coho and Chinook salmon have also been stocked experimentally.

But it is the sporty walleye especially that sports fishers troll for in May and June. At night these fish cruise in from the depths of the lake where they have spent the daylight hours. Walleyes are nocturnal (most active at night) and their large eyes, which look like cloudy, white glass marbles, are adapted to night vision. The walleye population has declined since the invasion of exotic zebra mussels after 1986. Since walleye do not like the water clarity caused by zebra mussels, their numbers have declined.

Its close relative, the blue pike, found nowhere else but Lake Erie, is now extinct. It used to inhabit the deeper, cooler waters of Lake Erie, but has not been seen since the 1950s.

Salt Water Ballast Brings Trouble to Fresh Water

The clean up of Lake Erie was a success, but international shipping has troubled the Great Lakes waters in recent years. Shipping cargo on the Great Lakes is a multi-million dollar business that includes over eighty ports on all five Great Lakes and the St. Lawrence River.

Ships arrive from all over the world, through the mouth of the St. Lawrence River and then through the interconnected Great Lakes to the northernmost and largest port at Duluth, Minnesota in Lake Superior.

The problem is, ocean going vessels carry sea water as ballast when they are not loaded to keep the ship stable. Upon arrival at a Great Lakes port, the hold was emptied of ballast water and then loaded with cargo of wheat or steel or whatever product it will carry. This practice led to serious problems in the Great Lakes since the seawater dumped from the holds carried the eggs or larvae of many species that do not belong in the fresh water of the Great Lakes such as the zebra mussel.

The invasion of zebra mussels was an unforeseen consequence of shipping on the Great Lakes. It is believed that the half inch long clam like creature reached the Great Lakes when a cargo ship emptied its ballast water into Lake St. Clair in 1986. The zebra mussel is a species native to the Caspian Sea region of the Soviet Union that had spread to Western Europe. With few natural predators in the Great Lakes, their populations exploded. Every year each female zebra mussel produces about 30,000 eggs. When fertilized, the eggs hatch into microscopic larvae that are carried with the current. When the larvae find a hard surface, they attach themselves and form a colony. Within three years the mussels had found their way into all of the Great Lakes. These invaders cling to every hard surface from reefs where fish spawn, to water intake pipes, to the hulls and motors of boats. The mussels multiply so rapidly that virtually all the hard surfaces in Lake St. Clair and Lake Erie are now covered with zebra mussel beds at least an inch thick.

Monroe, Michigan had to shut down its municipal water plant for three days when its intake pipes became coated with them. In 1989, thirty tons of them were found in a two and a half mile stretch of pipe at an Ontario water plant. Navigation buoys have sunk under the weight of millions of mussels.

Reefs where walleye and perch spawn are coated with mussels making them useless for native species. David Garon of Ohio State University says, "The zebra mussel is a keystone species. It has the power to restructure the entire ecological community."

It can strip water of algae and other phytoplankton. Native clams die when zebra mussels attach themselves to their shells in such numbers that they cannot open. Lately a diving duck called the scaup has been staying near Point Pelee well into December to feed on the zebra mussel. Twenty scaup used to show up near Point Pelee. In the fall of 1990, 13,500 scaup banqueted upon the zebra mussel. The freshwater drum, a fish also known as sheepshead also feed upon zebra mussels, but these predators cannot keep up with the zebra mussel's population explosion. Don Schloesser of the U. S. Fish and Wildlife Service says that their numbers double every day in Lake Erie.

Now the base of the food pyramids in all the Great Lakes has been affected by the zebra mussel, according to Tom Nalepa, a biologist who has been tracking the disappearance of diporeia, a high fat crustacean. Diporeia is an important food for medium size fish that larger fish such as walleye and salmon feed upon.

If we imagine that the food pyramid is made of bricks (plankton), and we keep removing bricks from the base of the pyramid, it is possible that the pyramid could topple.

The quagga mussel, a close relative of the zebra mussel, has also invaded the Great Lakes from the same area of the world as the zebra mussel, but unlike the zebra mussel that lives in shallow water, the quagga mussel's niche is deep cold water.

More Exotics

In 1990, more exotic fish were discovered: the round goby and the tube nose goby in the St. Clair River, Lake St. Clair and Lake Erie. They have now spread to all of the Great Lakes. These natives of the Caspian and Black Seas in Russia average four inches in length, have a black spot on their dorsal fins, and are able to hang onto the river bottoms with pelvic fins that act as suction cups.

Gobies probably reached the lower Great Lakes in the same way as the zebra mussels: in the ballast water of ships. Gobies are native to the same area the zebra mussels came from, the Black and Caspian Seas. Fortunately, zebra mussels are their favorite food.

How much effect these voracious little fish will have upon the out of control zebra mussels is still unknown. Zebra mussels and gobis have now invaded all of the Great Lakes and their connecting waters. In April of 1994, perch fisherman pulled up perch near South Haven in Lake Michigan that were feeding upon zebra mussels.

A new exotic to Lakes Michigan and Ontario is the fish hook flea, or cercopagis. It has a long tail spine like bythotrephes and reached the Great Lakes through shipping from other parts of the globe.

Since December 1992, it has been mandatory for sea-going ships to exchange ballast water well out of U. S. waters to get rid of stowaways, yet this may not solve the problem since there is still residue left in the holds and even ships with no salt water ballast may come into the Great Lakes with cargo, unload it, and then take on fresh water. The resting spores of organisms can hatch once they are exposed to fresh water. Even the hulls of ships can carry exotic species.

Tumors have been found in Lake Michigan zooplankton. Researchers are trying to find the cause and a solution to the problem.

The Great Lakes Fisheries Commission has recently found these exotic species in and around the Great Lakes: 59 plants including purple loosestrife that threatens wetlands; 25 foreign fish, 24 kinds of algae; 14 mollusks; six crustaceans; three benthic worms; three disease pathogens; two jellyfish; two insects; and one flatworm.

Of these new species, 55% are native to Europe and Asia and 13 from the Atlantic coast. Twenty nine percent of the exotics arrived in ballast water. Another 29% were introduced accidentally by aquarium or hatchery owners. Only ten percent swam up the Welland Canal.

Zebra mussels have improved the clarity of Great Lakes waters by acting as natural water filters; they filter plankton and water impurities at the rate of one quart of water each day for each zebra mussel. Divers report the water clarity in Lake Michigan used to be 10 feet but is now 45 to 90 feet.

By 1993, freshwater sponges, ephydiatia fluviatilis, a species native to the Great Lakes, were observed growing on zebra mussels and killing them. The sponges covered colonies of zebra mussels in a thin mat about one quarter of an inch thick. Perhaps improved water clarity and cleanliness resulted in the population upswing of freshwater sponges. Spongilla, freshwater sponges, have been in the

66

Great Lakes for thousands of years. According to Todd Petersen of Indiana Sea Grant, spongilla grew at a rate of two to three sponge colonies per square meter of water in 1992, but by 1993 10 to 15 colonies per square meter were found on the submerged Shedd Aquarium Ice Pier in Chicago and in other near shore areas of Illinois and Indiana.

Often zooplankton and phytoplankton form communities around zebra mussels and sponges. These include: hydra, bryozoans and attached algae as well as copepods, planaria, scuds and fairy shrimp, otherwise known as eubranchipus.

By 1953, silver chubs were nearly extinct in the Lake Erie ecosystem but they have made a come back after fifty years. This is good news since these small fish thrive on zebra mussels. Zebra mussels have been detrimental to other endemic fish except the sheepshead or freshwater drum.

According to Nicholas E. Mandrake, a research scientist with the Canadian Department of Fisheries and Oceans, silver chubs evolved to eat small clams and native mussels. He believes there will never be enough silver chubs to eliminate zebra mussels, but if they could make a dent, that would be pretty incredible.

Silver chubs are sensitive to pollution, so their return is good news for Lake Erie.

Pesky Exotic Zooplankton

Several types of zooplankton have also been dumped into the Great Lakes in ballast water: two of these are Eurytemora, an invader from saltwater, and the spiny tailed bythotrephes, invaders from European freshwater, a species of water flea with a huge appetite.

Researchers found that one of these half-inch long planktors can clear 1½ quarts of water of native water fleas known as daphnia that provide food for newborn fish such as chubs and perch. The introduced species has a spiny tail that makes it inedible for young fish, although bigger fish could handle it. Bythotrephes first were found in Lake Huron in 1984 and by 1986 had spread to Lake Erie and Lake Ontario. Now, like the zebra mussel, they are found in all the Great Lakes. They may have been carried from Europe in water ballast aboard empty grain freighters from the Soviet Union and then dumped into the lakes when the freighters loaded grain into their holds. This type of planktor are found in fresh water throughout northern Europe, but is not a problem there since all the plankton and fish there are adapted to it and it to them. When a new species is introduced, the results are often harmful to existing species.

It's as if hostile aliens from another planet were dropped in your hometown and then began to eat all the food in sight and inhabit all the buildings in town. Exotic species such as the European type of plankton take over because there is no species to keep their numbers in check.

Anglers find the pesky bythotrephes clinging to their fish lines. Nothing like this had ever happened before. Fish such as the ruffe, and the right eyed flounder usually found in salt water show up increasingly in the Great Lakes. Like byththepes, The ruffe displaces native species such as perch filling their niches, but the flounder has not been a problem.

Lake Erie changed from an "earthly paradise" in the 1700s to what some people thought was a dying lake in the 1950s, 60s, and 70s. After spending money to clean it up, nature showed its resiliency by again producing walleye and other wildlife in abundance. But the walleye declined due to water clarity.

Now over 140 exotic species, some introduced accidentally and some intentionally, challenge us to find new solutions.

Some of Lake Erie's Fish

Native: walleye, sucker, yellow perch, channel catfish, drum, blue pike (extinct), northern pike, small mouth bass, white bass, sturgeon, gizzard shad, emerald shiner

Introduced: goldfish, rainbow trout (steelhead), rainbow smelt, brown trout, alewife, sunfish, coho salmon, carp

6

Lake Ontario

"Each generation must deal anew with the raiders, with the scramble to use public resources for private profit and with the tendency to prefer short run profits to long run necessities."
–John F. Kennedy

Length: 193 mi/311 km
Breadth: 53 mi/85 km
Depth 282 ft. 86 m average 804 ft. 245 m maximum
Volume 393 cu mi/1,640 cu km
Water Surface Area 7,340 sq mi/ 18,960 sq km
Shoreline length 726 mi/ 1,168 km including islands
Elevation 246 ft/ 75 m
Outlet St. Lawrence River to the Atlantic Ocean
Retention/Replacement time 6 years
Population: 2,704,284 U.S. 5,446,611 Canada

Lake Ontario is deep, 804 feet at its deepest point, and its average depth is 282 feet. Of the five Great Lakes, only Lake Superior is deeper. Although deep, it is the smallest Great Lake in surface area, but holds a greater volume of water than shallow Lake Erie. Unlike

71

warm Lake Erie, Lake Ontario holds a large proportion of cold bottom waters.

On its way to Lake Ontario, the last in the flowing river of seas, water rushes down the Niagara River making a spectacular drop over Niagara Falls before flowing into Lake Ontario, the easternmost of the five Great Lakes. The Lake Ontario basin encompasses the incoming Niagara River, Niagara Falls, and numerous other lakes and streams that empty into the lake before the waters discharge into the St. Lawrence River.

Water that flowed through Lake Superior, Lake Michigan, Lake Huron, Lake Erie, and finally Lake Ontario flows out through the St. Lawrence River with its chain of more than 1,800 islands.

It takes six years for the water in Lake Ontario to replace itself. The Canadian shore of Lake Ontario is heavily populated and heavily industrialized: one in eight Canadians lives in the Lake Ontario basin. Its more sparsely populated opposite shore along the state of New York is used for farmland and resorts. There are no tall sand dunes or rocky cliffs along Lake Ontario. Its level shores were the first of the Great Lakes to be developed in the early 1800s since level land is suitable for farming or building.

Lake Ontario is classified as a mesotrophic lake which means it is in between oligotrophic and eutrophic. High numbers of algae growth on both ends of the lake show where the lake is eutrophic, a sign that the lake is aging before its time like a person who eats only junk food, and then suffers from poor health. Pollutants age a lake before its time. Pollution is nothing new to Lake Ontario since it has been exploited longer than any of the other Great Lakes, first by lumber mills and commercial fishermen, and then by farmers and manufacturers.

By 1898, its unique species of landlocked Atlantic salmon was extinct.

Lake Ontario's Last Landlocked Atlantic Salmon

The year is 1898. A forty pound Atlantic salmon fights her way upstream, through the thick sawdust of a lumber mill. Her belly bulges with eggs, and as salmon have always done, she tries valiantly to return to her traditional birthplace to spawn. The stones on the bottom of the stream are covered with mud and debris. The sawdust clogs her gills and by the time she lays her eggs, she can hardly breathe. No male follows her to fertilize the eggs.

She is the last landlocked Atlantic salmon in Lake Ontario; her eggs will never hatch. The mud covers them. In a week she is also dead. Landlocked Atlantic salmon in Lake Ontario are now extinct and have been since 1898.

Before saw mills clogged spawning streams with sawdust and mud and commercial fishermen caught too many of them in their seine nets, Lake Ontario's landlocked Atlantic salmon thrived. At some time in the distant past, these salmon swam 1,000 miles up the St. Lawrence River from the Atlantic Ocean, adapted to the fresh water of Lake Ontario, and became an important part of the ecosystem. They no longer returned to the salt water to live, but used Lake Ontario's tributaries to spawn.

By the early 1800s, European settlers arrived on Lake Ontario's shores, earlier in its history than the other Great Lakes, and these immigrants changed the lake's ecosystems profoundly. Commercial fishermen cashed in on a bonanza of fish resulting in a decline of the populations of Atlantic salmon after 1835. By the end of the century the native landlocked Atlantic salmon had disappeared.

Destruction of spawning streams by lumber mills, over fishing, and pollution caused its extinction.

Loss of Species

After the extinction of the magnificent landlocked Atlantic

salmon, further losses were recorded between1929 and 1975. Sixty-four fish species were recorded in the 1920s compared to 51 in the 1970s, a loss of 13 species (E. J. Crossman annotated list).

Among these were: native lake trout, lake whitefish, bloater chub, once abundant in Lake Ontario's deep waters, and sturgeon.

The kiyi, a distinct subspecies of cisco, found only in Lake Ontario is now extinct.

Once abundant, the sturgeon fed on the bottom of the lake with their vacuum like mouths. This biological niche is now filled by a non-native species: the carp, not nearly as interesting or valuable a fish as the prehistoric looking sturgeon, but carp can tolerate more pollution, and they produce more young.

Pollution in the last 40 years has prevented a comeback of large predator fish such as lake trout and lake whitefish.

When the predator fish at the top of the food chain were gone, or nearly gone, then small fish, invaders from the sea such as alewife and smelt exploded their populations without the large fish to keep their numbers in check. The lake trout once inhabited the deepest parts of the lake and migrated to the shallower parts; once these disappeared an important link in the food chain was broken. No large predator fish inhabits this deep-water niche now. Sometimes alewives are found in these depths, and a small fish called the slimy sculpin, but no large fish that preys on the smaller fish to move energy through this pathway from the deep parts of the lake to the shallow. The changes in fish populations are recorded by W. J. Christie in "A Review of the Changes in the Fish Species Composition of Lake Ontario" (*Great Lakes Fishery Commission*).

Before European immigrants arrived with commercial fishing, lumber mills, farming, and manufacturing, the fish in Lake Ontario were characteristic of a large, oligotrophic lake; its ecosystem was like a finely woven fabric with every thread contributing to the overall pattern. Today the fabric has been torn. After evolving for thousands of years and adapting to Lake Ontario's specific conditions, some species have disappeared, damaging the overall ecosystem.

Some niches in the ecosystem are filled with less desirable species of plankton, insects, fish, birds, and plants.

Small mouth bass, pumpkinseed, and rock bass live around the shallow shoals and islands of the eastern basin of the lake making their living by catching minnows, frogs, and insects. Carp and suckers have replaced some of these fish since they are more tolerant of pollution.

A niche is a place in the natural community where a living thing is adapted to the food chains and habitat. The place where a fish lives and eats and spawns is its niche. When a niche is vacated by one species, another species may move in, occupy the same space, eat the same food and use the same places to spawn.

Planted fish fill the niche once used by the native landlocked Atlantic salmon.

Planted Fish

After improving streams by cleaning up pollution, planting trees on their banks and removing dams, The Ontario Department of Game and Fisheries as well as the New York Department of Environmental Conservation planted rainbow trout, brown trout, Chinook and coho salmon, and these filled the ecological niche once inhabited by the native landlocked Atlantic salmon.

In 1983, nearly 100 years after the extinction of Lake Ontario's landlocked Atlantic salmon, the New York Department of Environmental Conservation planted a close relative of the native landlocked Atlantic salmon in the same streams. (Atlantic salmon were also planted in other Great Lakes.) After maturing in the open waters of Lake Ontario, the hatchery-raised Atlantic salmon returned to the New York streams in 1987, the same streams where they had been planted three years before as yearlings. Unlike conditions 100 years ago, the spawning streams are thick with other planted fish: brown trout, rainbow trout, Chinook and coho salmon.

Like the Atlantic salmon, these are anadromous fish, which means they are fish that return from a lake or ocean to spawn in the stream where they have imprinted the memory of their birth place. All fill the same niche in Lake Ontario.

American Eels Follow an Ancient Pattern

While anadromous fish such as the salmon live in seas or lakes and return to their birthplaces in a stream to mate and lay their eggs, American eels do just the opposite: they live in freshwater and then swim to the exact location where they hatched in the saltwater seas to mate. The mature American eel looks like a snake with a long dorsal fin and may live from five to twenty years. At about eight years, they make an incredible journey from the Great Lakes to their birthplace in the Sargasso Sea to spawn, a journey of thousands of miles through the Atlantic. When they reach the Sargasso Sea, a sluggish area filled with seaweed that lies between Bermuda and Puerto Rico, they spawn and die. Their eggs hatch into transparent, leaf like larvae that drift in the Gulf Stream feeding upon plankton until they reach the Gulf of St. Lawrence, a year's journey.

By this time they have reached a length of six inches and have become round-bodied young eels called elvers or grass eels. From the river's mouth they swim in thick swarms for a thousand more miles up the St. Lawrence River into Lake Ontario. A few ambitious American eels may reach other Great Lakes if they are lucky. Most of the elvers are gobbled by hungry fish or birds. Once commercially valuable, the American eel should not presently be used as a food fish by humans since they have picked up contaminants, mercury and mirex by scavenging the waters of the St. Lawrence River and Lake Ontario.

Unlike the parasitic lamprey eel, the American eel is a scavenger—it cleans up debris and recycles material. Every ecosystem needs recyclers to prevent it from becoming clogged with dead material. Nothing goes to waste in an ecological system when it is undisturbed. Human beings are learning to be less wasteful by recycling paper, plastics, metals etc.

Yet some chemical wastes do not break down for hundreds of years and cause problems to the environment. An illustration of this is the Niagara River.

The Niagara River, 37 miles long (59km) flows between the United States and Canada from Lake Erie to Lake Ontario, the easternmost of the five Great Lakes.

On the banks of the Niagara River, 250 toxic waste dumps hold chemicals; some poisons, a legacy from the past, are leaching into the river and then reach Lake Ontario where they enter food chains. One of the worst toxic dump sites was New York's Love Canal. In 1977, 1,000 families were evacuated from the Love Canal area because toxic fumes were leaking into their houses. The houses had been built on top of a toxic chemical dump. An unusually high number of birth defects and cancers afflicted these people. Now the contaminated area has been capped and contaminated creeks north of the site dredged.

In June of 1990, the government declared the Love Canal safe enough for people to move back, however this decision is controversial.

The Niagara River dilutes toxins because its strong current flows at 200,000 cubic feet per second. The problem is the toxins diluted in the Niagara River end up in Lake Ontario, the last in a flowing river of lakes: it receives the wastes from all of the other Great Lakes connecting rivers and tributaries in the basin as well.

Niagara on the Lake, a community at the mouth of the Niagara

River that drew its water from Lake Ontario, became alarmed at their health risks and built a pipeline to draw their city water supply from Lake Erie.

In the lower Niagara River, for instance, people are warned about eating American eel, rainbow trout, white suckers, coho salmon, small mouth bass, freshwater drums, white perch, lake trout, channel catfish, and Chinook salmon.

This is because of biological magnification: toxins gather strength as they move up the food chains. Every state around the Great Lakes has issued fish consumption advisories in certain areas. Researchers found tumors and heart disease in fish from Hamilton Harbor, on the west end of the lake. The bottom sediments in harbors such as this have polluted sediments, a difficult problem to solve since the process of removing bottom sediment might release some the toxins into the water.

Today quite a few people believe that if the environment can't handle a waste and break it down into harmless elements, it shouldn't be produced.

Once, Lake Ontario's deep cold-water ecosystem produced landlocked Atlantic salmon, lake trout, whitefish and many other species of fish. Then its inviting level shores were quickly built upon and settlers unsettled the natural order of life that had evolved since the Ice Age. The extinctions began.

Beluga Whales

In the last 50 years, toxic wastes became a threat to all living things in Lake Ontario and the waters it empties into. The toxins PCB and mirex have been ingested by about 500 white beluga whales that feed upon thousands of migrating American eels at the mouth of the St. Lawrence River. Mirex, an insecticide once produced on the shore of Lake Ontario has been banned since the 1970s, but its residues linger in the bottom sediments where eels feed. As a result of feeding upon the eels laden with toxins, the whales have developed tumors, cancers and reproductive problems and they die young. Aluminum smelter workers in the area have developed the same type of bladder cancer as the whales.

Pollution migrates through ecosystems, and in this case, from fresh water to salt. PCBs, DDT, chlordane, and toxaphene were also found in the flesh of dead beluga whales and they must be disposed of as toxic waste.

As in the other Great Lakes, biologists have experimented with planted fish in an effort to restore an ecological balance, but without changing the way we produce goods and dispose of wastes, Lake Ontario will not be a healthy lake for fish, birds, whales or people.

A nine year study of people who ate fish from Lake Michigan found that those who consumed more than 24 pounds of the fish each year, and had elevated levels of PCBs in their bodies, scored poorly on memory and learning tests. The study applied to all adults. Dr. Susan Schanz, a University of Illinois researcher, points out the risks of eating too much fish from the Great Lakes.

The International Joint Commission stated that toxic chemicals deleterious to the human condition must no longer be tolerated in the ecosystem.

Fish Found in Lake Ontario

Some Native species: Atlantic landlocked salmon (extinct) lake trout (extinct), lake whitefish (extinct), bloater chub (extinct) sturgeon (extinct) kiyi (extinct) smallmouth bass, pumpkinseed, rock bass, American eel, slimy sculpin, channel catfish, black bullhead, longnose gar, lake chub

Introduced or Accidental species: smelt, alewife, Chinook salmon, rainbow trout, brown trout, Atlantic salmon

7

Great Lakes Cycles

"There dwells the dearest freshness deep down things."
–Gerard Manley Hopkins

The life cycles of lake trout, mayflies, American eels, and other forms of life are intertwined with the changing cycles of the Great Lakes. This chapter is about various cycles that occur on the Great Lakes.

The Four Seasons

Summer

It's a windy summer day on the Great Lakes. White herring gulls and black sooty terns play on flowing currents of air. Raptors glide on airstreams: bald eagles, peregrine falcons, ospreys. The booms of starting cannons signal the starts of sailing regattas. On some beaches, sailboarders leap waves guiding their sails toward the beaches, then out toward the horizon again. Momentarily airborne, their colorful sails are like the wings of the birds sailing above them, yet from a distance they resemble colorful butterflies.

On beaches, people fly kites of many shapes and colors: red, blue, violet, yellow. The kites swoop and dance on the ends of their strings: dragon-shaped, or multiples of diamonds, rectangles and circles.

When the wind dies and all is still on the Great Lakes, herons wade in the coastal wetlands, occasionally spearing a frog or fish with their long beaks. On a sandy beach, the wet sand sings a high-

81

pitched tone when someone drags a toe or a shoe over it. These singing sands are composed mainly of fine textured quartz, about 80 percent, along with dark grains of magnetite and other granules of rock. Moving water has the ability to sort soils and rocks. The sorted grains of magnetite, therefore, can look like a dark stain on the water's edge. A magnet will pick up these grains and leave the quartz behind.

On the water's edge, a group of people builds an elaborate sand castle. They know the waves will wash it away in a little while, but for the time being, it is a work of art. Small children occupy themselves with digging holes and watching them fill with water.

On such a calm day fishing boats not far from shore would look as if they were set on a mirror, if it were not for the slight, undulating movement of the water. A kayak skims the still surface as the paddle dips rhythmically. Someone notices that the lake has a white cast on its surface. *What is it?* they wonder.

The Lakes' Self-Cleansing Abilities

In August a satellite coasting high overhead takes photos of the Great Lakes. Huge sections of all five Great Lakes have lightened in color. It is the late summer Whiting Effect: for a few weeks the surface water changes to a milky white color, the result of naturally occurring calcium carbonate in the water that becomes visible under certain conditions. The Whiting Effect is one way the lakes cleanse pollutants from their waters. Here is how it works: millions of tiny particles of calcium carbonate which are usually dissolved in the water become solidified when surface waters are warm and the phytoplankton in the top 25 meters of water have been active. Phytoplankton plays a key role in the Whiting Effect since they alter the acidity/alkalinity (pH) of the water. Then the naturally occurring calcium carbonate that saturates the Great Lakes becomes visible, giving the lakes a white sheen.

As the white calcium carbonate particles accumulate due to the water temperature and the actions of phytoplankton, they become heavier and heavier and then finally sink deeper into the lakes where they redissolve in the cooler temperatures and higher water pressure deep in the lake. As the calcium carbonate dissolves, it removes pollutants, including metals, from the top layers of the lake. Calcium carbonate absorbs these elements well.

In the summer, most of the aquatic life, phytoplankton, zooplankton, as well as fish such as perch live in the lakes' sunny upper layer: 25 meters. Understanding the Whiting Effect may help scientists understand how pollutants move into and out of Great Lakes food chains.

Other Ways Water Cleanses Itself of Impurities

Moving water is self-cleansing whether in a flowing stream or in the motion of the waves, or the turnover of water in lakes. The winds over the Great Lakes cause wave action helping the water to cleanse itself as dissolved oxygen (DO) mixes with moving water. Sunlight on water also cleanses some impurities by breaking them down into their elements.

These natural processes cleanse the water of impurities as long as too much pollution is not dumped into the lakes all at once, or as long as chemicals that do not break down easily are not added to the water through air pollution, leaching into the water through the ground, or directly from tributary streams or lake side farms, municipalities or industries.

Indicators of Clean Water

Some types of insects indicate how clean a body of water is. Where water is clean, mayflies, caddis flies, stone flies and hellgrammites live and provide food for a wide array of fish and birds. Where water is polluted, the midge fly larvae, rat tailed maggots, and aquatic earthworms survive in the bottom sediments of the lakes because they require less oxygen.

Mixing and Stratification of Water

Anyone who has ever waded out into a lake on a hot summer day has noticed how the water suddenly changes temperature: warm near shore, then cold. Imagine yourself on a sandy shore on the beach. It's a hot day in August and you can't wait to get into the water. As you splash through the shallow water, it feels warm and pleasant around your legs, but as you wade out waist deep, it suddenly feels cold. Standing chin-deep, you can feel warm water around your neck and cold water around your waist. When you dive under, it's really cold on the bottom.

In summer, water in lakes becomes layered with the warmest layer on top, a middle layer that changes temperature rapidly and then at the deepest level, an even colder layer of water.

Why the Water is Different Temperatures in Summer

In early summer the water in lakes warms and currents mix the warm water with the colder water below. Later on, as the water on the top becomes warmer, and warmer, it becomes lighter and cannot mix with the denser cold water below it. As the summer sun continues to warm the top layer of lake the water begins to stratify into layers. The surface layer is called the epilimnion. Since warm water is not as dense or heavy as cooler water, it floats on the upper layer.

The cooler middle layer of water is called the thermocline, and as swimmers know, it becomes rapidly cooler as one dives deeper. Some Great Lakes fishermen who own underwater digital thermometers measure the temperature of the water to find the thermocline and then lower their lures to this depth, for the change in water temperature offshore is the place where steelhead, salmon, and lake trout often feed. Even without a thermometer, the change in water color tells fishermen where a change in water temperature is: the water changes color from greenish to deep blue. Sometimes sports fishers find the good fishing spot by seeing where debris is floating. The sinking water action causes floating objects to accumulate on top of the place where the water abruptly changes temperature.

The bottom of the lakes is cooler still, and contains less and less oxygen as the summer progresses. This is because there is no mixing of the top waters containing more oxygen while the water is stratified. Stratified water cannot mix.

Surface water temperatures among the Great Lakes vary a great deal in the summer. On Lakes Michigan, Huron and Erie, the epilimnion may reach 80° F, while the surface water in the middle of the deeper and most northern Lake Superior may be less than 50° F.

Summer Stratification of Lake Water

Epilimnion: light warm surface water

Thermocline: rapid transition of temperature

Hypolimnion: heavy cool water on the lake bottom

Fall Turnover of Water

On a cold November night with no clouds, the reflections of the moon and stars sparkle on the calm surfaces of the lakes, and the silhouette of a vee shaped string of geese migrating southward crosses the salmon colored moon. Cold north winds have cooled the Great Lakes waters.

As the air cools, the water becomes cooler and cooler. When water reaches 39.2° F, it reaches its greatest density. Waves rolling in on the beach look heavier, almost like boiling sugar water as it just begins to thicken. The fall turnover of water is about to occur, an important event in the natural cycle of the Great Lakes. When surface lake water reaches 39.2° F, its maximum density, the water sinks since the surface water is heavier than the water below.

The sinking top layer of water causes the lake water to turn over. The fall turnover of water in the Great Lakes is important because oxygen poor water in the deeper areas of the lakes mixes with surface water containing more dissolved oxygen (DO). This keeps the bottom from becoming depleted of oxygen.

Bottom dwelling fish and plankton need dissolved oxygen in water just as we need oxygen in air. When the layers of water turn over, there are no longer three layers of water since mixed water results in uniform temperatures.

Winter Stratification

The water stratifies into layers again in winter as the top layer of water is cooled below 39.2° F or 4° C. When it becomes colder than 39.2° (its densest) it is less dense, therefore lighter and stays at the top. Ice is lighter than water.

Lakes freeze from the top down and not from the bottom up because the water on the bottom is the heaviest, 39.2° F or 4° C. This denser water does not freeze since the freezing point of water is 32° F.

Since lakes do not freeze all the way to the bottom, fish and plankton continue to feed, though some become less active in the winter. Great Lakes fish such as the whitefish, lake trout and perch continue to explore the waters for food while some warm water fish in Lake Erie such as bass and bluegills may sink lower in the waters and feed little. Catfish and bullheads hibernate in the mud at the bottom.

The Great Lakes are so large that they seldom freeze all the way across or even part way across, but it has happened.

In mid-February of 1979, four of the five Great Lakes froze all the way across. This was the first year this had happened in the recorded history of the National Weather Service.

Shore Ice

On the eastern side of Lake Michigan, ice begins to form along the shore, usually in December. The first crystals of ice begin where water meets the shore. Ice crystals must have something solid to cling to in order to form. This is why ice does not form out in the middle of lakes first, but begins to build along the shoreline. When the temperature plummets and the water takes on a steely sheen, ice gains a toehold on the shore. Crystals of ice build into a formation known as an ice foot. The ice foot builds out into the lake and eventually becomes a strong seawall that will protect sandy beaches from erosion during fierce winter storms.

An ice volcano will form where there is a weak spot in the ice foot. The repeated action of waves spraying through a hole in the ice creates a cone shaped volcano. When more ice builds out into the lake and waves can no longer reach the volcano, it becomes inactive.

Wave action also forms ice ridges that run parallel to the shore. Ice pushed by the relentless waves buckles and rides up on adjacent ice forming rows of ridges. Ice balls looking as if they had been fired from polar cannons float on the restless water and bounce up on the ice ridges during storms. Water sprays and freezes the ice balls in place so the ridges resemble a wall built of fieldstones—a wall with the glazed luster of fused glass.

People who walk along the shore often see large, flat, round cakes of ice floating near shore and sometimes as far as the eye can see. When sheets of ice break off they are in shapes like a broken plate glass window, but then the continual knocking together by the rolling action of the waves causes the shapes to become rounded and curled up at the edges like gigantic pancakes. Sometimes the pancake ice looks like bumper cars crashing into each other like a wild carnival ride.

A walk along the eastern shore of Lake Michigan in winter is a fascinating sight with ice volcanoes spouting ice water, pancake ice, and ice ridges with frozen water in the gullies between them. Ice balls bounce and roll and their clattering sound mingles with the swoosh of the spray, the clinking of pieces of ice in the water, the roar of wind, and crashing of waves. Some of the formations remind people of grottos, caves, castles, and thrones. But anyone who ventures out onto the shore ice in winter should beware. Quirks of winds and waves and the shape of the lake bottom causes the shore ice to change from day to day and even change from minute to minute.

It seems as if a sleight of hand magician were playing tricks with water, wind, and ice. One of these tricks is to strand wildlife or people on a floating cake of ice. Pack ice shifts and changes continually. As long as the stationary shore ice stays in place it protects sandy beaches from erosion during winter storms.

During thaws, a white churning mass of slush ice can be seen. As the weather warms in March, the ice begins to break up. The stationary ice foot that formed first on the beach in December is also the first ice to melt in March. Offshore winds loosen the stiff white collar of ice. A spring storm with strong, steady west winds will push ice up onto the shore. Heavy winds cannonball huge ice chunks high onto the beach. Ice breaking up makes eerie sounds—cracks and groans caused by the tremendous pressure of huge ice masses about to move. The walls of ice crumble in the March sunshine splashing into the lake like undermined castle walls.

Spring Turnover of Lake Water

Before the ice melts in spring, the temperature at the interface of the ice and water is 0° C or 32° F and the water temperature at the bottom of the lake is 4° C or 39.2° F. When the sun warms the water above 0° C it becomes more dense and sinks, and colder water from below replaces it. Lake water then mixes, resulting in water of equal density from top to bottom. Winds blowing across the surface mix the waters.

This mixing is called the spring turnover. The Great Lakes' waters turn over and mix in the spring and fall and stratify in the summer and winter. As water conditions change, living things also change: the plankton, the fish, and their food webs. Living things adapt to seasonal changes in their environment; changes in light, temperature, dissolved oxygen, acidity/alkalinity (pH) nutrients, and other factors.

Lake Levels: Another Natural Cycle

There are seasonal changes in the Great Lakes waters: the stratification of water in the summer, the fall turnover, winter stratification and spring turnover. There are also changes that occur over longer periods of time. Lake levels rise and fall over the years, a fact some people did not know when they built homes, warehouses, and even skyscrapers in Chicago too close to the powerful waves of the Great Lakes.

1500 Years of Changing Lake Levels

Geologists have found that lake levels in Lake Michigan and Huron have fluctuated between highs of around 585 feet and lows of 572 feet for the past 1,500 years. Fifty feet of beach can disappear in just a few hours during a storm when waves undercut a sand bank and wash it away, especially when lake levels are high.

Record lows were set in 1964. People bought beachfront property and built during the time of low water, not understanding that changes in lake levels are normal. The amount of water in the Great Lakes rises and falls periodically.

What were once broad, sandy beaches when the houses were built crumbled in 1985 and 1986 when lake levels rose to a higher level than anyone could remember. Houses and cottages were undermined and toppled into the lake, yet this could have been predicted since accurate records of lake levels have been made since 1900.

During fall and spring storms, waves washed beachfront property away while people frantically placed sand bags and built expensive sea walls in an attempt to keep the water away. During a 1987 February storm, twenty-foot waves leaped over the Chicago seawall and streets, for blocks inland were flooded. New apartment buildings built too close to the shoreline were undermined by water making expensive beachfront real estate unfit for habitation.

During the high water levels in the mid 1980s, four of the five Great Lakes, Superior, Michigan, Huron and Erie were at their highest level of the century, the highest that had been recorded since 1900.

Undermined houses were condemned around Lake Erie. In the next few years, the lake levels dropped again leaving broad sandy beaches. Some boat docks were left high and dry.

The amount of precipitation, rain and snow, along with the rate of evaporation from the sun cause the lakes levels to rise and fall. Some of the processes influencing water levels are still not completely understood by scientists.

Lake levels have been rising and falling ever since the Great Lakes were formed by the glaciers in the Pleistocene Age. Water levels also have annual cycles: low in January or February and high around June or July. The seasonal differences range between one and two feet.

Evaporation accounts for the greatest loss of water from the basin. Over a long-term average, it is believed that evaporation and precipitation balance. The average precipitation (rain, snow, sleet) averages 31 inches per year. Groundwater also recharges the lakes.

To some extent, man-made locks on the Soo affect lake levels of Lake Superior. Hydroelectric dams affect Lake Erie's water levels and locks at Lake Ontario's outlet affect its level.

The water diverted out of Lake Michigan at Chicago lowers the level of Lakes Michigan and Huron by 6 centimeters (2.5 inches).

Recently, Canadian and U. S. experts (International Joint Commission) were asked to study the water levels of the Great Lakes. Their conclusion was that human interventions have relatively minor impacts on fluctuations in comparison with natural forces, and that efforts to control Great Lakes water levels are probably futile. Compared to the power of natural forces, engineers' efforts do not have much effect.

Tides may affect lake levels, but not to the same degree as in the Atlantic and Pacific Oceans. The tides in the Great Lakes are caused by the sun and the moon, but they are scarcely noticeable: only 1½ to 3 inches.

Seiche

Of more concern than tides are short-term changes in lake levels caused by a seiche wave that can cause sudden damage. In 1954 a seiche wave on Lake Michigan swept people off of a pier in Chicago and at least seven lives were lost.

The highest seiche recorded on the Great Lakes was on Lake Erie in 1942: at Buffalo the lake stood 13.5 feet higher than at Toledo 250 miles to the west. In 1844 a sudden wind shift caused a great seiche wave on Lake Erie to sweep into the city of Buffalo, New York causing loss of life and boat wrecks in the harbor.

A seiche wave is caused by the gradual rising or lowering of the water caused by wind or barometric pressure changes. A seiche may last for a few minutes to several hours. Water is forced from one end of the lake and piled up on the other. Once the wind stops blowing or the pressure changes, the water oscillates back and forth across the lake causing an alternating rise and fall of levels at lake ends. It is like water sloshing from one end of the bathtub to the other.

Lake levels can be affected by storms. Since the Great Lakes lie in the middle of the continent, they are subject to great extremes of weather conditions. The region lies at a junction of paths of lows from several areas of cyclone development and late fall storms are likely. Great Lakes storms often come from the following regions: Texas, New Mexico, the Central Rocky Mountains, the Great Plains, and the Pacific Southwest.

Winds on the lakes are usually from the west. They can blow from any direction, though, and affect the currents in the lakes.

Lake Effect

The lakes themselves affect the weather since water stores heat in the summer and stores cold in the winter. This is an advantage for growers of specialized crops such as blueberries, cherries, apples, and grapes. The heat retained by the lakes in the summer makes a longer harvest season in the fall and the cold retained by the lakes in the winter keeps fruit trees from budding too early in the spring. The lakes moderate the weather near them, creating favorable growing conditions, especially along the east coast of Lake Michigan, and the New York coast of Lake Erie.

Hydrological Cycle Powered by the Sun

The Great Lakes hold about 20 percent of the fresh surface water in the world. They are an important part of the total global hydrological cycle. After hundreds of millions of years, Planet Earth's original supply of water is still in use.

Powered by the sun, water recycles continuously. During the Pleistocene, a large amount of water remained locked into glaciers, and then melted to form the Great Lakes. Some of this glacial water seeped into aquifers deep underground. An aquifer is a water-bearing layer of rock such as sandstone, limestone or gravel. These underground reservoirs lie under the land everywhere.

Aquifer water follows gravity downhill moving slowly through pores in the rock formation. The water in some aquifers recharges Great Lakes waters by slowly moving through the ground and into the lake. Many homes and communities draw their water directly from underground aquifers. They are an important part of the Great Lakes ecosystem.

Eventually, every drop of water moves through the system, pumped up from the Earth into the air by the sun, then falling as rain, and flowing again into saltwater and freshwater seas. The hydrologic cycle uses more energy in a day than man has generated throughout history. Water is never completely destroyed or used up.

The molecules of water in a fish or a human being were once clouds, dew, rain, snow, or ice. Without water there would be no life.

A human being is a porous sac of water; only one third of the human body is made of other substances. The water dinosaurs drank may now be an ice cube in a glass of lemonade or in the leaves and petals of a thousand marsh marigolds.

The rain that fell upon Paleo Indians now rises as mist over Lake Superior and frosts the white pines and balsams in the early morning sunlight. Of all the surface water on Earth, 95% is salt water and only 5% is fresh water. Fresh water is precious.

Sand Dune Cycles

Along the Great Lakes, and especially on the eastern shore of Lake Michigan, are the largest freshwater sand dunes in the world. It was here that the father of ecology, Henry Chandler Cowles, made observations about the rapidly changing plant life that led to the science of ecology.

In 1899 he published *The Ecological Relation of the Vegetation on the Sand Dunes of Lake Michigan*. In this paper he showed the

93

mutual relationships between plants and their environment.

"Ecology is a study in dynamics," he wrote.

The word dynamic means change. The Great Lakes are dynamic. Sand dunes are dynamic, making them a living laboratory for the study of ecology.

Here is how the dune ecosystem changes with time:

0-20 years beach grasses
20-50 years cottonwood, beach grasses, cherry, willow, herbs
50-100 years Increasing variety of shrubs, trees, and herbs
jack pine may dominate
100 years black oak may be among the first forest dominants: oak and hickory
beech and maple climax forest

Succession

One group of plants replacing another is called succession. With the climax forest, the dunes have produced a diverse community of plants and animals that are part of the Great Lakes' ecosystem. Since the dunes were a gift of the glacier 13,000 years ago and the west winds, and the moving waters, we cannot replace them.

Beach grasses and other plants keep the dunes in place. Dunes are of more value to the whole ecosystem as dunes rather than as industrial sand or real estate. They protect inland areas from wind damage since wind blowing off the lake will glance off of a tall dune and rise up into the air. They also protect inland areas from flooding.

Dune plants are hardy—able to live through harsh summer and winter weather, but they cannot stand up to off the road vehicles or heavy foot traffic.

Building houses on dunes may cause wind erosion when the

plants stabilizing the dunes are removed. This is called a blowout and it forms a saddle shaped or U shaped depression in a stable sand dune. In order to protect Michigan's coastal sand dunes, the state government passed a law in 1989 that will prevent development that would be harmful to the dune's ecology or the mining of sand for industrial purposes. Certain subsequent governments have not enforced this law.

The intent of the law was to protect the dunes we still have left. In the past, irreplaceable dunes were trucked away load by load since the fine sand along Lake Michigan is useful for forming molds in manufacturing.

8

Problems and Possible Solutions

"Who is speaking for the water of the Earth?"
—Oren Lyons

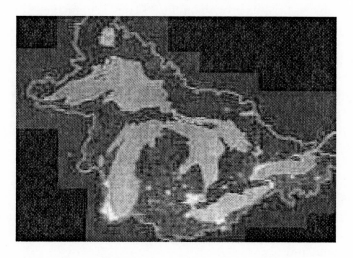

The credit for this picture goes to EPA Atlas

Population

Night satellite pictures show the shorelines around northern Lake Superior, Lake Michigan and Lake Huron are dark at night while the heavily populated areas on the southwest side of Lake Michigan and the shores of Lake Erie and Lake Ontario show up as bright blazes of light. There are over 33 million people living in the Great Lakes basin in the United States and Canada.

Geometric Growth

The population of the world doubled between 1950 and 1987:

97

only 37 years. Some have called the population explosion the greatest environmental problem.

The growth of human populations may be compared to certain types of pond weeds that double each day. Their growth begins slowly and ends rapidly. For instance, if it takes thirty days for the weed to completely cover the surface of the pond, its surface would be half covered on the 29th day. Although its growth was hardly noticeable at first, its growth on the 29th day is dramatic: from half of the pond to all available space on the pond's surface in just one day. Like pond weed, human populations are slow starters but fast finishers.

By 1650, the human race on Earth numbered about 500 million. By 1800, population reached 1 billion and after only 130 years, 2 billion. It took only 30 years to reach the third billion, 15 the fourth billion and 12 the fifth billion.

By Oct. 12, 1999 there were 6 billion people in the world. By 2025, there may be 8.5 billion and by 2050, 12.5 billion if the current rate of increase continues. Never before have human populations around the globe increased as rapidly as they are increasing now.

In 1798 Rev. Thomas Malthus published *Essay on the Principles of Population*. In it he observed that plants and animals have the potential to expand to fill millions of worlds in the course of a few thousand years but lack of space and nourishment (such as a small pond or the surface of the earth) prevents this from happening. This is why populations cannot expand indefinitely. Every population stabilizes or reaches a limit and then falls.

As we can see from space photographs, there is the same amount of land, air, and water on Earth as there has ever been, yet many more people along with more buildings, automobiles, and factories. Forests are being cut, and wetlands drained to provide land for growing populations.

Other species compete with humans for space (habitat) and are often the losers. Loss of species affects the health of the planet since diverse species indicate a healthy ecological system. Thousands of species from plankton to fish to birds to trees and wildflowers preserve the planet upon which we depend. If it were not for the green plant life producing oxygen, this planet would be as lifeless as the other planets in our solar system. Plant and animal life are interconnected and the human race is a part of the whole and flowing interconnected ecosystem.

Greatly increased human populations along with inventions such as automobiles, and manufacturing processes that cause pollution have caused new problems since the Industrial Revolution.

As human populations grow, ecological problems grow, as we have seen around the Great Lakes, yet with some foresight, many problems can be solved or prevented.

In years to come Great Lakes states and provinces will need to find ways to prevent too much water from leaving the Great Lakes watershed. Water poor states and countries outside of the Great Lakes watershed have their eyes on the fresh water. Water used in the Great Lakes watershed returns to the lakes. Water diverted outside the watershed may cause harm to the ecosystem. The Great Lakes are large, but fragile.

Offshore drilling for oil and gas is not permitted in the Great Lakes. The eight governors of the states bordering the Great Lakes ban oil drilling in the Great Lakes because they are so vulnerable to oil contamination.

Yet some oil exploration companies have drilled under Lake Michigan from on shore sites by means of directional drilling and want to explore for more oil under the Great Lakes. So far twelve wells have been drilled from offshore using directional drilling to go under the rock underlying the Lake Michigan basin. The first was in 1979 and the most recent, in 1997. There has been so much citizen opposition that this practice has been temporarily halted.

Many people believe this is circumventing the intent of the agreements among the state governors. Directional drilling for oil has the potential for destroying the world's greatest source of fresh surface water. Oil rigs on shore with the capability to drill under the lakes have an uncertain safety record.

Gambling with Lake Michigan, a lake with an outflow that takes nearly 100 years, could do great harm.

New York State has banned both directional drilling and offshore drilling for gas and oil in Lake Ontario. Canada has allowed 55 wells in Lake Erie. These wells use directional drilling under the lake's basin; the wellhead is on land.

Accidental oil spills in the Great Lakes have the potential for far more serious damage than an oil spill at sea because the water in the Great Lakes takes a long time to circulate through the system. An oil spill would affect the whole ecosystem from the microscopic plankton to the eagle with a seven-foot wingspan. It would affect the people who depend on Great Lakes water for domestic, agricultural and manufacturing purposes.

The Greenhouse Effect

Water levels of the Great Lakes may become much lower in the future due to the greenhouse effect. The greenhouse effect might change the climate of the Earth as people burn more and more fossil fuels (coal, oil, gas) producing carbon dioxide. This in combination with cutting down forests that produce oxygen could have bad results.

The increase of carbon dioxide along with other "greenhouse gases" such as methane, nitrous oxides, and chlorofluorocarbons, will trap heat from the sun, gradually warming the Earth. Although no one knows for sure whether this will happen, people around the world are taking the possibility seriously. To combat global warming, the U. S. committed to phasing out production of chlorofluorocarbons by the year 2000.

Trees and other plants help to absorb tons of greenhouse gasses, but more trees and plants are felled each year than are replanted. Trees help absorb carbon dioxide: a single tree absorbs up to 48 pounds per year, an acre of trees up to ten tons a year.

An organization called "Global Releaf" would like to get communities involved in planting trees. On Earth Day many people planted trees to help restore oxygen, and absorb greenhouse gases. They also thought of ways to use less energy; less energy used, less fossil fuel burned.

The land, the water, the air and their communities of living creatures are changing ecosystems we participate in. Ecosystems that have taken thousands or even millions of years to evolve are sometimes damaged overnight by the activities of human beings who do not foresee the consequences of their actions.

No one foresaw how the ecosystems would be affected by certain long lasting pesticides and how we would nearly lose whole species such as the bald eagle and the peregrine falcon. Eagles and peregrines are at the peak of the food pyramid, even higher on the pyramid than human beings since they only eat meat.

We can correct mistakes before it is too late; the elimination of DDT is a good example. People in Michigan became concerned about the effects of DDT and solved the problem through the democratic process. The first city to ban DDT in Michigan was Grand Haven. Citizens persuaded their city council to stop spraying elm trees on city property with DDT.

Seeking a broader solution, citizens sought a statewide ban by taking the problem to their state representatives in Lansing, Michigan. Their efforts succeeded and the Michigan legislature passed a law banning the use of this pesticide in Michigan in 1969.

Wisconsin and New Jersey, alerted by Rachel Carson's book, *Silent Spring,* were also among the first states to ban this harmful pesticide.

By 1972, Congress passed a law banning the use of DDT and pesticides like it in all fifty states. Canada Banned DDT in 1990. The democratic process works. What it takes is concerned citizens working toward solutions.

DDT is still used in some countries outside of the U. S. A. and Canada. Migrating birds such as warblers and peregrine falcons that winter in Central and South America are affected by pesticides there. Sometimes wind currents carry sprays for thousands of miles before they drop to earth again in rain. With their great surface area, 94,000 square miles, the Great Lakes receive airborne pollutants from around the globe in rain or snow or as dry particles.

Today PCBs, a group of synthetic chemicals that were phased out beginning in 1976, are the principal toxic chemical found in Great Lakes fish, according to Tiernan Henry, a Sea Grant water quality specialist. These toxins show up in the fat of fish. PCBs are suspected of causing human health problems.

An EPA report showed that 90% of PCBs reached Lake Superior through the atmosphere; 58% to Lake Michigan and 63% to Lake Huron. The PCBs deposited from the atmosphere in Lake Erie and Lake Ontario are less, but PCBs flow into them from other sources including the upper Great Lakes.

An ecosystem is a complex pattern of relationships among living things and their environment. Food pyramids and food chains are models showing how everything is connected to everything else from the microscopic bit of algae to the fish, to the eagles and falcons. We are part of this flow. We must learn to live in harmony with the natural world: for the sake of all living things, we must be aware of the consequences of our actions.

The land, the water, the air and their communities of living creatures are changing ecosystems we participate in.

Toxins

DDT, Dioxins, and like chemicals are extremely harmful to the life in the Great Lakes waters and the air and land surrounding them.

Such products should not be produced since they are too hazardous and pose unacceptable risks. Planting coho, Chinook and other types of trout and salmon in the Great Lakes brought sports fishers flocking to their shores. Anglers need to be aware that these fish bioaccumulate PCBs, mercury, lead, cadmium, and other toxins, especially in the fatty portions of their bodies.

Some persistent wastes released into the environment in past years still linger in the Great Lakes sediments, their tributary streams, groundwater, and their food chains.

In the past, water pollution problems were simpler. People worried about water born diseases such as typhoid. Today with the increase of chemicals and byproducts of manufacturing, the Great Lakes cannot flush out toxic materials before they become part of the food chains. Only one percent of Great Lakes water reaches the Atlantic Ocean.

The rest recycles through the air, soil, and water in the Great Lakes region along with some persistent pollutants.

The U. S. and Canada verified that there were 362 compounds with a high potential for toxicity in 1987. Eleven are deemed critical by the International Joint Commission, and we do not know all of the effects these have on ecosystems. In 1987, the Great Lakes Water Quality Agreement was updated and signed by Canada and the United States. This agreement calls for "control of the sources of emissions of toxic substances and the elimination of the sources."

According to ecologist Barry Commoner, "It doesn't do to produce the pollutant and then try to grab it back with controls. Progress occurs through certain changes in the way we produce our goods."

Some manufacturers have found ways to change their methods in order to keep toxins out of the environment. Some recycle wastes rather than discharging them into the environment and actually save money by recycling. About 30,000 chemical compounds are used in the Great Lakes basin and an additional 1,000 new chemicals are developed each year.

The best way to control toxins is to prevent them from reaching the environment in the first place. Zero discharge policies are hotly debated between businesses accustomed to doing business in the old way and policy-making groups with an eye to the future. One serious source of pollution in the Great Lakes is pulp and paper mills that use chlorine to bleach paper. Chlorine combines with pulp to form a variety of toxins including dioxin harmful to human beings, fish, and wildlife.

Other processes could be used to whiten paper and thereby eliminate these toxins. Changes in manufacturing processes could eliminate the problem.

According to the Environmental Protection Agency, there are 43 Areas of Concern—the most polluted places around the Great Lakes: 26 located entirely within the U. S.; 12 located entirely within Canada and five shared by both countries. Finding the best way to clean them up and finding the money to do so is a difficult problem. There are many loopholes in laws regulating pollution. The Lake Michigan Federation, a group of concerned citizens, has taken Federal Agencies to court to cause them to enforce their regulations.

Zero Discharge

In 1978 the Great Lakes Water Quality Agreement between the United States and Canada promised to achieve zero discharge into the Great Lakes to prevent pollution. So far, this has not been achieved, but it is a goal to work towards. Participation by citizens is very important in the process of working toward good changes.

Toxic Air Pollution

In recent years research has shown how much pollution reaches the Great Lakes from the air. Although virtually banned in 1982, toxaphene, an insecticide sprayed on crops in the south, showed up on a lake on Lake Superior's Isle Royale showing the far reaching effects of airborne pollutants. David Hales, former Director of the Michigan State Department of Natural Resources, observed that Congress must pass national legislation to rid the air of toxic clouds of smoke.

According to EPA statistics in 1990, U. S. industries pump 3 billion pounds of toxic substances into the air each year threatening health and life wherever the toxins are carried on streams of air and deposited by precipitation.

In the 1980s scientific evidence grew showing that at least half of all the toxic pollution entering the Great Lakes comes from the air. The Great Lakes are susceptible to global air pollutants because of their enormous surface area. Airborne debris such as DDT sprayed as far away as South America to control malaria reaches the Great Lakes.

Fish in polluted parts of the Great Lakes have developed tumors on their lips. Small amounts of toxic substances in the water magnify through the food chain causing birth defects, cancers, and mutations in fish and birds.

Presently, we don't know the long term effects on people because people live much longer than fish or birds and researchers haven't had long enough to study what happens when people eat food at the end of the food chain or the top of the food pyramid as compared to fairly short-lived fish or birds.

The International Joint Commission's report on the Great Lakes Water Quality stated: "We have concluded from wildlife and laboratory animal information that persistent toxic substances in the Great lakes Basin ecosystem pose serious health risks to living organisms. Sixteen Great lakes wildlife species near the top of the food web have had reproductive problems or declines in populations at one time or another since 1950. In each case, high concentrations of contaminants have been found in animal tissue.

Together with available human data, the information leads us to conclude that persistent toxic substances in the Great Lakes environment also threaten human health. It would be unwise and imprudent not to take immediate action."

Nuclear Power

There are 37 nuclear power plants in the Great Lakes basin. Plutonium, the most toxic substance known, is a by-product of nuclear power plants. It is extremely hazardous because of its high radioactivity: for half of its quantity to decay, it takes 24,360 years. Our aging Nuclear Power Plants on the Great Lakes presently have nowhere to store plutonium except on their property.

On the Palisades Nuclear Power Plant property on the shore of Lake Michigan near South Haven, eight 100 ton casks stand on a concrete slab only 150 feet from the waters of Lake Michigan. This distance varies with the seasonal changes in water levels.

The 16½ foot high casks are eleven feet in diameter and weigh 100 tons. They consist of a steel basket encased in 29 inches of concrete and stand on a concrete slab. Palisades may eventually have 25 casks. Plutonium is so toxic that it could mean an end to life as we know it in the Great Lakes region. Low-level radio nuclides like tritium escape into the ecosystem from these plants and like other toxins, radioactivity magnifies through food chains. The nuclear power plants are aging and must be phased out. Their radioactive wastes pose an urgent problem that will have to be solved soon. No one has solved the problem of how to store plutonium safely. Uranium mining on the Canadian shore of the Lake Huron Basin also poses hazardous waste problems.

The other nuclear power plants on the shores of the Great Lakes also lack a sensible solution. Nuclear waste should be stored in a permanent place where there is little or no chance of reaching water.

Former Attorney General of Michigan, Frank Kelly, stated the storage of nuclear waste "the greatest threat to the Great Lakes in the history of mankind."

The Great Lakes' value can't be measured in dollars and cents only, for who can measure the loss of health or put a price on the beauty of a place?

In 1978, Oren Lyons, Chief of the Onondaga Turtle Clan, delivered a speech at the Cathedral of St. John the Divine in New York City. Here is an excerpt from his talk:

> We went to Geneva—the Six Nations, and the great Lakota nation—as representatives of the indigenous people of the Western Hemisphere. We went to Geneva, and we spoke in the forum of the United Nations. For a short time we stood equal among the people and the nations of the world.
>
> And what was the message that we gave? There is a hue and cry for human rights—human rights, they said, for all people. And the indigenous people said: What of the rights of the natural world? Where is the seat for the buffalo or the eagle? Who is representing them here in this forum? Who is speaking for the water

of the earth? Who is speaking for the trees and the forests? Who is speaking for the fish—for the whales—for the beavers—for our children? We said: Given this opportunity to speak in the international forum, then it is our duty to say that we must stand for these people and the natural world and its rights; and also for the generations to come. We would not fulfill our duty if we did not say that. It becomes important because without the water, without the trees, there is no life.

What We Can Do

Echoing this thought in 1991, the Science Advisory Board made up of 18 scientists from the United States as well as Canada asked the International Joint Commission for the Great Lakes to develop a code of ethics for the Great Lakes ecosystems. Moral choices are decided in terms of what is right or wrong rather than what will make the most profit for a business.

With a greater appreciation of the ecosystem, voters must insist their elected representatives take action, to help make the air, water, and land as clean as possible so that the whole web of life may thrive. People must take personal responsibility for Planet Earth by making sure they do not contribute to the problems in their hometown or city.

On Planet Earth, the Great Lakes are absolutely unique.

The decisions we make in our daily lives, and the choice we make in who represents us in our government may affect generations to come. The Great Lakes system is a treasure. Understanding their natural processes and understanding the dynamics of what we do is essential to these life-giving waters.

The way to solve pollution problems is to think globally and to act locally.

Picture yourself as an astronaut looking down from a spacecraft at this beautiful planet, the Earth. From space, it is easy to see that everything is connected to everything else. The great masses of swirling clouds travel over the continents, drop rain, and sometimes along with the rain, pollutants. The lakes, rivers and seas are interconnected. In order to control global pollution problems they must be controlled at their source.

In order to act locally, some communities, both adult groups and school age students have adopted a stream. They have observed the places where pollution might be occurring, then they have spoken out against pollution in their communities, city councils or other government agencies. Local groups of people are in the best position to observe what is happening to their local stream.

Local citizens can help develop cleanup strategies and local pollution prevention programs. The problem is too important to leave to government officials and industries alone.

Legislation to curb pollution needs to be on a global level as well as on national, state and local levels since everyone is a part of the global whole and flowing air, water, and land ecosystems.

The view of planet Earth as seen from a satellite in outer space shows the continents, deep blue oceans, and white swirling clouds of vapor. The five Great Lakes show their distinct, interconnected shapes; unique bodies of fresh water.

Of all the planets our satellite cameras and telescopes have probed, only Earth looks inviting or habitable. A famous photograph taken from the moon shows Earth rising against a barren moonscape where nothing lives. In the foreground we see jagged rock, but rising in the distance is Earth with its liquid medium: water. Water and life are inseparable. Where there is life, there is water; where there is water, there is life.

All nations as well as all living things share the water and air supply that is the planet's life support system; therefore we all share a responsibility for the cleanliness of the air, water, land and its living webs of life. Air and water never stop to show a passport, but circulate freely around the globe. The great swirling airstreams and water systems we can see from a satellite circulate continually.

If we thought of the Earth as an apple, a layer of life-supporting air, soil, and water would only be as thick as the apple's skin. Life on Earth is only possible as long as our limited life support system works.

We are all challenged to use our knowledge, creativity and common sense to keep the Great Lakes great. Can you think of ways to think globally and act locally?

Works and Experts Consulted

Dr. Chilton Prouty, geologist, M.S.U. Interview 1/22/87

Pringle, Laurence, Rivers and Lakes, *Time Life Books*, 1985, Alexandria, VA.

Luttenton, Mark, Water Resources Institute, Grand Valley State University, interviews.

The Great Lakes, An Environmental Atlas and Resource Book, Environment Canada, U.S.

Environmental Protection Agency, Brock University, Northwestern University 2001.

Schneider, Keith. Progress Not Victory on Great Lakes Pollution, The New York Times, May 7, 1994 p. 1

Emilia Askari. Waves of Change, Detroit Free Press, May 11, 1993

Arno, Karlen. Superior, New York, Harper & Row, 1974

Fahnenstiel, Gary L et. al. Importance of Picoplankton in Lake Superior, NOAA Great Lakes Environmental Research Laboratory, U. M. Ann Arbor MI 1986

Deephouse, Wm. Fisheries Division, Michigan DNR, Lake Superior redfin lake trout, 1990 interview

Dr. Karl Z. Morgan, director of health and physics at Oak Ridge National Laboratories. "Toxic Pollution and the Great Lakes", Greenpeace 13, July/Aug 19

Peterson, Todd. Indiana Sea Grant (spongilla)

McBeath, Sandy and Wolf, Earl, naturalists. The Gillette Nature Center, Norton Shores, Michigan interviews

The Muskegon Chronicle. "Huge Lake Sturgeon Increasing in Number," July 12, 1987

Dennis, Jerry. Fish Flies, Michigan Natural Resources, May June 1990, vol 59, no. 3

The Great Lakes Reporter, vol 7, No 6, Nov./Dec. Center for the Great Lakes

McClane, A. J. Field Guide to Freshwater fishes of North America, Holt, Rinehart & Winston, N. Y. 1978

State of the Great Lakes, Michigan Department of Natural Resources

Seines to Salmon Charters 150 Years of Michigan Great Lakes Fisheries, Extension Bulletin E-1000 May 1977, Michigan Sea Grant Program

Sloat, Bill. "Biologists Discover Lake Erie Silver Trove," The Plain Dealer, 2-8-02

Pistis, Chuck. Seagrant, (zebra mussels, quagga mussels, spongilla) interview 1998

Crossman, E.J., Van Meter, Harry. Annotated List of the Fishes of the Lake Ontario Watershed, Technical Report No. 36, Great Lakes Fishery Commission, June 1979

Coker, R. E. This Great and Wide Sea, Harper Torch books, New York, 1962 p. 263

Barry, James P. The Fate of the Lakes, Baker Book House, Grand Rapids, MI 1972

Peterson, Joan M. and Dersch, Eckhart. A Guide to Sand Dune and Coastal Ecosystem Functional Relationships bulletin, MSU, CES, U of M and Michigan Sea Grant.

Lake levels profile, Living with the Great Lakes, Environment Canada's Ontario Weather Centre

Elliott, Margaret Drake. Dune Grasses, Michigan Natural Resources Magazine July, August, 1985

Cowles, Henry Chandler. "The Ecological Relation of the Vegetation on the Sand Dunes of Lake Michigan," 1899

Great Lakes Notebook, Public Information Office, Great Lakes Basin Commission, Ann Arbor, MI 48106

Ehrlich, Paul R. Anne H. "Population, Plenty and Poverty" National Geographic, vol 174, no 6, December 1988

Segerberg, Osborn Jr. *Where Have All the Flowers, Fishes, Birds, Trees, Water and Air Gone?*

Center for the Great Lakes Sept/Oct 1989 vol 6, no.5

EQ 2001 Annual Report to Congress on global air toxics

Magnuson, Ed. " The Nuclear Scandal," *Time*, Oct. 31, 1988

Parabola. "Our Mother Earth" vol vi no 1, 1981, p.93.

Samuels, Mike, Zina, Hall. *Well Body, Well Earth*, Sierra Club Books, San Francisco

Tenth Biennial Report of Great Lakes Water Quality July 2000

Commoner, Barry. Dioxin Fallout In the Great Lakes, June 1996, Center for the Biology of Natural Systems, Queens College, CUNY, Flushing, New York, www.gc.edu/CBN/dxnsum.html

Peterson, R.E. Early life stage toxicity of...dioxin, www.sciencenews.org

Steingraber. *Sandra, Living Downstream,* Addison Wesley Publishing Co. 1997

Mills, Edward, Director, Cornell Biological Field Station, Senior Research Associate, Department of Natural Resources

Greil, Roger. Lake Superior State University, e-mail interview about the Pinook

Pearce, Jeremy. "Lake Fish Tied to Memory Loss" The Detroit News, July 12, 2001

Printed in the United States
29402LVS00001B/158